WILLIAM RIMMER

BROCKTON ART MUSEUM/FULLER MEMORIAL
October 6, 1985–January 12, 1986

THE CLEVELAND MUSEUM OF ART
February 25–April 20, 1986

THE BROOKLYN MUSEUM
June 6–July 20, 1986

William Rimmer, *Alexander Hamilton*, 1865, granite. Gift from Thomas Lee to the City of Boston. Located on Commonwealth Avenue mall, between Arlington and Berkeley streets.

WILLIAM RIMMER

A Yankee Michelangelo

Essays by JEFFREY WEIDMAN, NEIL HARRIS, and PHILIP CASH

With a Foreword by THEODORE E. STEBBINS, JR.

Distributed for the Brockton Art Museum/Fuller Memorial
by University Press of New England
Hanover and London, 1985

*UNIVERSITY PRESS OF
NEW ENGLAND*

BRANDEIS UNIVERSITY
BROWN UNIVERSITY
CLARK UNIVERSITY
UNIVERSITY OF CONNECTICUT
DARTMOUTH COLLEGE
UNIVERSITY OF NEW HAMPSHIRE
UNIVERSITY OF RHODE ISLAND
TUFTS UNIVERSITY
UNIVERSITY OF VERMONT

Printed in the United States of America

Front cover illustration: *Sunset/Contemplation*, reproduced by permission of the Manoogian Collection

Back cover illustration: *Dying Centaur*, reproduced by permission of the Museum of Fine Arts, Boston

LIBRARY OF CONGRESS CATALOGING IN PUBLICATION DATA

Rimmer, William, 1816–1879.
   William Rimmer, a Yankee Michelangelo.

   Catalog of the exhibition held at the Brockton Art Museum, 6 Oct. 1985–12 Jan. 1986; the Cleveland Museum of Art, 25 Feb.–20 Apr. 1986; and the Brooklyn Museum, 6 June–20 July 1986.
   Bibliography: p.
   1. Rimmer, William, 1816–1879—Exhibitions.
I. Weidman, Jeffrey, 1945–   .   II. Harris, Neil, 1938–   .   III. Cash, Philip.   IV. Brockton Art Museum.   V. Cleveland Museum of Art.   VI. Brooklyn Museum.   VII. Title.
N6537.R546A4   1985   709′.2′4   85–70907
ISBN 0–934358–14–1 (pbk.)

CONTENTS

FOREWORD

The last major exhibition of the work of William Rimmer occurred in 1946. Yet the words with which Juliana Force began her Foreword to that catalog remain accurate today. She wrote: "William Rimmer was one of the most remarkable figures in American art—a powerful draughtsman, a learned anatomist, a great teacher, a highly imaginative painter, and the most gifted sculptor of his time in this country. Yet his work is seldom seen and his name little known to the public."

Though the last forty years have seen a reevaluation of American art, Rimmer's place has stayed much as it was. Today we would still judge the artist as Mrs. Force did, and it is still true that his work is seldom seen and his name little known. Rimmer remains a particularly elusive figure: today it is hard to know him, and it is harder still to categorize his work or to place it within the context of American art and American style.

To consider Rimmer is to encounter one anomaly after another. For example, he is best known today as a painter, his reputation resting largely on just one canvas, *Flight and Pursuit*, which the artist gave away the year it was painted and which began to be singled out by critics only in the mid-twentieth century. Though this is a remarkable work, the fact is that Rimmer was less accomplished and less significant as a painter than as a sculptor and draughtsman.

Another anomaly: Rimmer was unusually sophisticated, yet he was sloppy and careless in his art. With his aristocratic aspirations, his long artistic apprenticeship, his medical studies, and his general learning, he drew on a wide variety of sources from Leonardo and Michaelangelo to Milton and Blake; yet his paintings have suffered from the use of poor materials, and

in sculpture he seemed hardly to be aware of the most basic use of armatures. One explanation is that he seems to have taken great pride in his ability to execute a painting or a sculpture with great speed.

Rimmer's drawings, on the other hand, are simply fanatical in their craft and their detail, and they demonstrate an obsession with anatomy and particularly musculature. The illustrations to his two impressive books, *The Elements of Design* (1864) and *Art Anatomy* (1877) succeed on their own as fine works of art; yet they may also share the weakness of all of Rimmer's work, for, as brilliant and evocative as they are, they nonetheless fail to suggest a deeper truth. Despite his romantic mind-set and his obvious passion for art, Rimmer seldom evokes real passion.

Rimmer's contemporaries were such artists as George Caleb Bingham, Martin Johnson Heade, and John F. Kensett, yet his concerns were quite different from theirs: whereas Bingham and the others gave a realist-romantic expression to American myth and to the American land, Rimmer struggled to develop in painting and sculpture a figurative style based on European culture. In this aim he belongs to the younger generation of Eastman Johnson, Thomas Eakins, and William Morris Hunt, all artists who made use of extensive European training in establishing successful careers in this country during the 1860's.

Clearly Rimmer was at a disadvantage in terms of both time and place. Given his "noble" French background, he must have felt very isolated. During the 1830's and 1840's, as he grew to middle age in the halcyon years of nativist American art, he must have felt equally frustrated as he tried to form a new style based on European memories—for he was far ahead of his time—without benefit of the advanced European training (such as Johnson and Hunt received) that would have made his ambitions plausible.

Moreover, Rimmer lived in Boston during the weakest decades in its artistic history. He might have looked to the aging Washington Allston as a role model until that artist's death in 1843, but then there would have been few artists to nurture and prod him until William Morris Hunt (1824–1879) returned to Boston in 1862. Hunt was everything Rimmer must have wished to be: attractive, debonair, well-connected socially, and a prolific master of the new French style. Rimmer may have had more genius, but Hunt made more of his talent.

Like Hunt and Eakins, Rimmer was renowned as an inspiring and dedicated teacher, and his students found him "exciting and encouraging, kind and caring." But outside of the classroom his personality became a serious problem. He was described by one contemporary as "conceited and overbearing," and by another as "stubborn, unmanageable, thin-skinned." He possessed a hot temper, and would explode at a slight provocation. One observer noted that he was "his own worst enemy," and this is undoubtedly true: then as now, an artist who is difficult and unpleasant is likely to have a hard time.

Nonetheless, Rimmer was fortunate in that the special qualities of his art always won him a few champions. Early on, he was patronized by Stephen Higginson Perkins of Boston, and his loyal admirer Truman H. Bartlett produced a superb, lavishly illustrated book (*The Art Life of William Rimmer*) in 1882. In 1880, the year following his death, the Museum of Fine Arts, Boston, honored him with the second one-artist show in its young history, just following one devoted to Hunt. Further exhibitions were held in Boston in 1916 (on the centenary of his birth) and in New York and Boston in 1946–47, the latter organized by another great champion of this artist, Lincoln Kirstein. Rimmer's work has been included in the major surveys of American art since the Metropolitan Museum's centenary exhibition of 1970, and he is increasingly recognized as "the most gifted sculptor of his time in this country."

In 1985 the Brockton Art Museum and Dr. Jeffrey Weidman join a distinguished and historic company in becoming the champions of Rimmer's work for our time. We are all in their debt.

January 28, 1985

Theodore E. Stebbins, Jr.
John Moors Cabot Curator of American Art
Museum of Fine Arts, Boston

ACKNOWLEDGMENTS

The Brockton Art Museum/Fuller Memorial is proud to present *William Rimmer: A Yankee Michelangelo,* the largest and most important in a series of shows organized by the Museum to highlight the work of significant artists associated with southeastern Massachusetts. A new and thorough look at Rimmer is very timely. The last major exhibition of the artist's works was organized by Lincoln Kirstein and the Whitney Museum of American Art and held at the Whitney in 1946 and at the Museum of Fine Arts, Boston, in 1947. The Brockton exhibition catalog is the first publication on Rimmer in almost forty years, and the first ever to reproduce so many of his works in color.

During the past several decades, a number of previously unknown or thought-to-be-lost works by Rimmer have been discovered, and more works have become accessible to the public through exhibition, reproduction, and movement from private to public ownership. For example, in 1967 Kennedy Galleries copyrighted an edition of fifteen bronzes of the *Dying Centaur,* many of which are today in public collections. In 1977, The Art Institute of Chicago acquired Rimmer's magnificent bust of *St. Stephen,* a work that had been essentially inaccessible to the public since its Boston exhibition in 1860. The Museum of Fine Arts, Boston, chose to include Rimmer's *Flight and Pursuit* in its splendid exhibition *A New World: Masterpieces of American Painting, 1780–1910,* which introduced this example of the artist's vision to European as well as American audiences. Most recently, a previously unknown oil, *Sunset/Contemplation,* has come to light and has been generously lent to the show.

Although Rimmer's diaries have been lost and the prove-nance of his works is often sketchy, we are indebted to several persons whose efforts to preserve his works and research his life story have provided us with a considerable body of material, among them Truman H. Bartlett, who wrote *The Art Life of William Rimmer* (1882); Caroline Hunt Rimmer (d. 1918), the artist's youngest daughter, and her niece, Edith Rimmer Durham Simonds (Mrs. Henry Simonds; d. 1935); Lincoln Kirstein; and the many dealers and collectors who have been interested in Rimmer's art. In New York, Kennedy Galleries and Hirschl and Adler Galleries have actively promoted Rimmer's work. In Boston his artistic legacy has been of particular interest to the Vose Galleries, to the Fayette Gallery (no longer in existence), and to Giovanni Castano (1896–1978), who had galleries first in Boston and later in Needham Heights.

Special congratulations and sincere thanks are due our consulting curator for the exhibition, Dr. Jeffrey Weidman of Oberlin College, who through his dedicated research, his Ph.D. dissertation for Indiana University, his lecturing, and his published articles has contributed tremendously to our understanding of Rimmer. Dr. Weidman has been the mainstay of this exhibition, guiding us in the selection of works, preparing the catalog entries and the introductory essay, and successfully dealing with countless questions and problems along the way.

This exhibition would not have been possible without the encouragement and cooperation of scholars and museum professionals who have furthered the project at every step. We are deeply indebted to Dr. Mark D. Altschule, Director of the Boston Medical Library, who originally suggested the exhibition and put us in touch with Dr. Weidman, and to Mr. Richard J. Wolfe, Curator of Special Collections at the Library, who provided research materials and guidance over the past four years. At the Museum of Fine Arts, Boston, Curators Clifford Ackley and Jonathan Fairbanks have given generously of their time and expert advice, as have Sue W. Reed of the Department of Prints, Drawings, and Photographs and Carol Troyen of the Department of Paintings.

I wish especially to acknowledge the very great help of Theodore E. Stebbins, Jr., John Moors Cabot Curator of American Art at the Museum of Fine Arts, Boston, for his unflagging support of the exhibition as well as for his thoughtful Foreword to this volume. We are grateful also to Dr. Neil Harris of the University of Chicago and Dr. Philip Cash of Emmanuel College, Boston, for their insightful essays.

We greatly appreciate the cooperation of the two other museums that are hosting the exhibition, The Cleveland Museum of Art and The Brooklyn Museum, who have made it possible for a broad national audience to enjoy Rimmer's work for the first time.

The exhibition and catalog would not have been possible without generous financial support on many levels. The exhibition and interpretive materials were funded by grants from the National Endowment for the Arts and the National Endowment for the Humanities. The catalog, a key aspect of the project, which will remain in circulation long after the show itself has been dispersed, was produced with the support of a generous grant from the Eleanor Naylor Dana Charitable Trust.

In closing, I must thank the staff of the Brockton Art Museum/Fuller Memorial, and above all the Museum's former Director, Marilyn Friedman Hoffman, under whose guidance the exhibition was conceived and so ably begun. Over the past four years each staff member has contributed to the formulation of this exhibition, and it has been truly the cooperation of the entire staff that has made the project a success. I would like to thank in particular Elizabeth Critchley Haff, Curator, and Nancy Padnos, Jacalyn Cahill, Julie Thompson, Linda Woolford, and James Swan for their outstanding work.

Joseph L. Kagle, Jr.
Director
Brockton Art Museum/Fuller Memorial

LIST OF LENDERS

Achenbach Foundation for Graphic Arts, The Fine Arts
    Museums of San Francisco
Addison Gallery of American Art, Phillips Academy
American Antiquarian Society
Boston Medical Library in the Francis A. Countway
    Library of Medicine
Morton C. Bradley, Jr.
Brigham Young University
Museum of Art, Carnegie Institute
Chelsea Public Library
The Art Institute of Chicago
The Corcoran Gallery of Art
Mr. Richard Cramer
Mrs. Seth T. Crawford
Detroit Institute of Arts
Mr. Richard L. Feigen
Richard L. Feigen & Co.
Mr. Joseph Feldman
Mr. Marshall Field

Foxborough Historical Society
Harvard University Art Museums (Fogg Art Museum)
Kennedy Galleries
Leonard and Corrine Lemberg
Clarence and Mildred Long
Manoogian Collection
Mead Art Gallery, Amherst College
The Metropolitan Museum of Art
The University of Michigan Museum of Art
Museum of Fine Arts, Boston
National Museum of American Art,
    Smithsonian Institution
The Art Museum, Princeton University
Smith College Museum of Art
Samuel J. Stein, M.D.
Wadsworth Atheneum
Mr. S. Grant Waters
Worcester Art Museum
and private collections

CHRONOLOGY OF WILLIAM RIMMER

Jeffrey Weidman

1816	Feb. 20, birth of William Rimer, Liverpool, England.
1818	Thomas Rimer emigrates to Nova Scotia, followed by his wife and son.
1819	Rimer family settles in Aroostook County, Maine.
1825	Rimer family settles in South Boston. Thomas Rimer first appears in the Boston Directory, listed as a "labourer."
1827	Boston Directory listing gives spelling of Thomas's last name as "Rimmer."
c. 1828–1832	Early art work of William Rimmer.
1831–32	Portraits, signs. Gypsum sculpture of *Seated Man* [Museum of Fine Arts, Boston].
1837	Works at Thomas Moore's and Daniel Jenkins's lithographic shops. Early lithographs. Member of Fire Engine Company No. 1 and the City Guards.
c. 1838	Partnership with Elbridge Harris, sign painting of *Cromwell at the Battle of Marston Moor*. Paintings for the Jesuit Church of St. Mary's, Endicott Street, Boston.
1838	William Rimmer and George Nelson listed in Boston Directory as soap manufacturers at 72 Congress. Exhibition of Rimmer's gypsum statuettes at Colton's art store on Tremont Street.
c. 1839	Exhibition of *After the Death of Abel* is financial failure.
1839–46	Portraits in Randolph and Brockton.
1840	Dec. 17, marries Mary Hazard Corey Peabody in Boston.
c. 1841–1847	Studies medicine sporadically with Dr. Abel Washburn Kingman, Brockton.
1841–45	Itinerant portrait painter in the areas of Randolph and Brockton.
1841	Birth of first son, William, Jr.
1843	South Boston: paintings for SS. Peter and Paul, Broadway; meets Dr. W. T. Parker; dissecting at Massachusetts Medical College, Mason Street. Death of William, Jr., and birth and death of second son, Thomas.
1844	Birth of third son, William 2nd.
1845–55	Settles and lives in Randolph. Friendship with Father John Roddan.
1846	Oct. 24, birth of first daughter, Mary (died 1891).
c. 1847	Commissions from Father Roddan for paintings for Old St. Mary's, Randolph.
1847	Death of third son, William 2nd.
c. 1848	Begins to practice medicine.
1848	Thomas Rimmer is moved from South Boston to Concord.
1848–52	Friendship with Amos Bronson Alcott and his family and with Ralph Waldo Emerson, Concord.
1849	Birth of second daughter, Adeline A. (died 1908). Marble bust of daughter, *Mary Rimmer* [Boston Medical Library].
1851	Oct. 10, birth of third daughter, Caroline Hunt (died 1918).
1852	August 3, death of Thomas Rimmer in Concord.

1854   Birth of fourth daughter, Louisa F.

1855   Death of fourth daughter, Louisa F. Short, fruitless prospecting venture in Lowell. Moves family to Chelsea, where he practices medicine. Before the year is over, moves and settles in East Milton.

1855–63 Lives in East Milton.

1857   Birth of fourth and last son, Horace W.

1858   Begins sculpting in granite. Friendship with Stephen Higginson Perkins begins.

1859   Death of last son, Horace W.

1860   Oct. 6, record of Rimmer's visit to the Sculpture Gallery of the Boston Athenaeum. Early Nov.– early Dec. (four weeks), execution of granite bust of *St. Stephen* [The Art Institute of Chicago]. Dec. 12, review in the *Boston Daily Journal* of the *St. Stephen*'s exhibition at Williams & Everett's art gallery, Boston.

1861   Feb. 4–June 10, execution of the *Falling Gladiator* [National Museum of American Art]. Nov., begins giving art anatomy lectures in Boston.

1862   Jan., joins the Boston Art Club. Perkins sails for Europe; original *St. Stephen* and cast of *Falling Gladiator* sent to him.

1863   Cast of *Falling Gladiator* in Salon des Refusés, Paris. Oct. 14, begins series of lectures at Lowell Institute, Boston. Gives up medical practice. Moves from East Milton to Chelsea. (It is possible that this move took place in early 1864.)

1864   Continues lecturing at Lowell Institute through June. Feb. 10, circular signed by illustrious Bostonians to raise support for private art school. School opens in Boston in March under Rimmer's direction, and continues through the spring of 1866. Publication of *Elements of Design*. Clay models of *Alexander Hamilton and Hawk-Headed Osiris*.

1865   Plaster *Hawk-Headed Osiris* exhibited at Childs & Jenks art gallery, Boston. Aug. 25, granite statue of *Alexander Hamilton* officially unveiled on Commonwealth Avenue. Granted Membership in the Star of Bethlehem Lodge, Chelsea. Fall, lectures on artistic anatomy at Harvard University. May have visited New York City during the fall.

1866   Jan., lectures on artistic anatomy at the National Academy of Design, New York City. Meets Peter Cooper. Lectures at Cooper Union and eventually accepts Cooper's offer to become Director of the School of Design for Women at Cooper Union, to begin in the fall. Summer, commissions from Domingo Faustino Sarmiento for marble busts of *Horace Mann* and *Abraham Lincoln* [both, Museo Historico Sarmiento, Buenos Aires]. Busts delivered in Feb. 1867. Before leaving Boston, resigns membership in Boston Art Club.

1866–70 Director, School of Design for Women, Cooper Union, New York City, terms Oct.–May of each year. Returns with family to Chelsea June–Sept. each year.

1868   June, Cooper Union classes attacked in *New-York Daily Tribune*. Plaster *Human Head (to Osiris)*. Fall, association with the American Photo-Sculpture Company of New York.

1869   Growing conflicts with Peter Cooper and Abram Hewitt at Cooper Union. May, exhibition at Cooper Union of *Dying Centaur* [Museum of Fine Arts, Boston].

1870   Oct., quits Cooper Union and returns to Boston. Rejoins Boston Art Club. *Fighting Lions* executed between Nov. and spring 1871. Dec. 20, membership canceled in Star of Bethlehem Lodge, Chelsea.

1870–76 Art anatomy classes in Boston.

1871   16 lectures at National Academy of Design, New York City. 12 lectures at Technological School, Worcester, Mass. *English Hunting Scene* [Museum of Fine Arts, Boston] painted. Oct. 3, Daniel Chester French begins classes with Rimmer in Boston; French's studies with Rimmer continue into 1872. Oct. 24–Dec. 19, 12 lectures in Providence.

1872   Jan. 22–Apr. 8, 12 lectures (second series) in Providence. Feb. 9, lectures on art anatomy at Yale School of Fine Arts, New Haven. Dec., *Flight and Pursuit* [Museum of Fine Arts, Boston] exhibited in Boston and Providence.

1872–73 Dec. 28–Mar. 15, 12 lectures (third series) in Providence.

1874–75   October, takes charge of night drawing school, Chelsea; continues into 1875. Member of School Committee, Chelsea. Lectures at the Free Industrial Drawing School.

c. 1875   Gives short course of lectures to artists meeting in L. G. Schirmer's room in Studio Building, Boston. Gives lecture on light to group of Boston photographers. Lectures and instructs occasionally at Miss H. M. Knowlton's Young Women's Art School.

1875   Model of *Faith* for Pilgrim Monument, Plymouth.

1875–76   October, takes charge for second time of night drawing school in Chelsea; continues into 1876. Declines re-election to Chelsea School Committee. Nov.–Jan., one lecture a week at home of Mrs. John Murray Forbes, Milton. Dec. 10–Feb. 25, 10 lectures at Normal Art School, Boston.

1876   Jan., works (e.g., *Gladiator and Lion* [Reynolda House] and *Fighting Lions* plaster) included in exhibition at Boston Art Club. Summer, Union, N.H., executes *Art Anatomy* drawings [Museum of Fine Arts, Boston]. Paints *Sunset/Contemplation* [Manoogian collection].

1876–77   Nov.–Jan., one lecture a week at home of Mrs. John Murray Forbes, Milton.

1877   Feb., works included in Review Club exhibition, Chelsea. Entire year, including summer, lectures on anatomy at Museum of Fine Arts' School, Boston. Plaster *Torso* [Museum of Fine Arts, Boston] and painting of *The Shepherd* [Boston Medical Library]. *Art Anatomy* published.

1877–78   Oct. through mid-June, lectures on anatomy at Museum of Fine Arts' School, Boston.

1878   Works on Albany mural designs for William Morris Hunt. Contributes print of *The Poor Man Has Nothing to Lose* [private collection] to *The Porcupine*.

1878–79   Oct. through mid-Apr., lectures on anatomy and modeling at Museum of Fine Arts' School, Boston.

1879   Revised edition of *Elements of Design* published with new section VI on form. End of spring, breakdown. Moves to home of his daughter Adeline and her husband, George Durham, in South Milford. Dies Aug. 20, aged 63 years and 6 months. Buried in Milton Cemetery.

1880   May through mid-Nov., *Exhibition of Sculpture, Oil Paintings, and Drawings by Dr. William Rimmer*, Museum of Fine Arts, Boston: approximately 150 works shown.

1882   Publication of Truman H. Bartlett's *The Art Life of William Rimmer: Sculptor, Painter, and Physician*.

1883   Feb., exhibition and private sale, 95 of Rimmer's works at J. Eastman Chase Gallery, Boston.

1905   Rimmer Memorial Committee formed by three former associates of Rimmer, William R. Ware, Daniel Chester French, and Edward R. Smith, to gather funds and arrange for bronze casting of *Dying Centaur*, *Falling Gladiator*, and *Fighting Lions*; they are assisted by the sculptors Augustus Saint-Gaudens and Gutzon Borglum. A cast of each sculpture acquired by Metropolitan Museum of Art between 1906 and 1907. A second cast of *Gladiator* acquired by Museum of Fine Arts, Boston, in 1908.

1913   Four unidentified drawings by Rimmer included in International Exhibition of Modern Art, popularly known as the Armory Show, in New York City and Chicago.

1915   Two paintings—*Angel in the Garden* [whereabouts unknown] and *At the Window* [National Museum of American Art]—included in Panama-Pacific International Exposition, San Francisco.

1916   Feb. 17–Mar. 1, approximately 135 works included in Centennial Exhibition, commemorating Rimmer's birth, at Museum of Fine Arts, Boston. No catalogue or checklist was printed.

1921   June 18, Gutzon Borglum publishes illustrated, enthusiastic appreciation of Rimmer's art in *New York Evening Post*: "Our Prophet Unhonored in Art."

1946–47   95 of Rimmer's works included in exhibition *William Rimmer, 1816–1879*, organized by Whitney Museum of American Art and Lincoln Kirstein (Kirstein wrote the catalog essay and entries). At Whitney, Nov. 5–27, 1946; at Museum of Fine Arts, Boston, Jan. 7–Feb. 2, 1947.

Part I ESSAYS

ILL. 1. William Rimmer, c. 1878. Photograph by J. J. Hawes. *Courtesy of the Boston Medical Library.*

WILLIAM RIMMER

Jeffrey Weidman

William Rimmer is one of the most intriguing, singular, and outstanding figures in American art. Perhaps the most gifted sculptor in America during the nineteenth century, he was also a painter of compelling and evocative images and a powerful and imaginative draftsman. A man of science as well as of art, he practiced medicine and was a learned anatomist. He was an inspired lecturer, who taught several of the next generation's major artists, and also a poet, author, musician, and inventor. His art and writings demonstrate familiarity with contemporary areas of philosophical thought and experience such as Transcendentalism and Spiritualism. He created the first nude sculpture in America (*Seated Man*, cat. 2), and probably the first granite carvings for other than utilitarian purposes (*Head of a Woman*, cat. 4, and *St. Stephen*, ill. 2, p. 38). Through his study of artistic anatomy, Rimmer fashioned a personal grammar of form in which the male nude became a metaphor for themes of heroic struggle. Certain of Rimmer's paintings (e.g., *Flight and Pursuit*, cat. 29, and *Sunset/Contemplation*, cat. 36) place him securely within the subjective, idealistic tradition in American art with artists such as Washington Allston, Elihu Vedder, and Albert Pinkham Ryder. On the whole, his art is not easily compartmentalized.

William Rimmer was born in Liverpool, England, on Feb-

ruary 20, 1816, and died at the age of 63 on August 20, 1879, in South Milford, Massachusetts. He came to the United States when he was two years old and never returned to Europe. He was raised in poverty and spent most of his life eking out a living for himself and his family. He made shoes, painted portraits, practiced medicine, and taught anatomy. He was virtually unknown as an artist until he was 45 years old.

Although a self-taught amateur in many respects, Rimmer was familiar with Europe's artistic traditions and more skilled at assimilating them than the majority of his contemporaries, especially in sculpture and drawing. His work also shows a knowledge of more recent artists like William Blake, Washington Allston, Antoine-Louis Barye, and Jean-Léon Gérôme, and an awareness of contemporary scientific and pseudo-scientific areas of investigation, among them photography, physiognomy, phrenology, typology, comparative anatomy, and Darwinian thought. Unlike many autodidacts Rimmer absorbed these many influences without imitating them. Far from being derivative, his works exhibit creative assimilation of their divergent thematic and formal sources.

Partly because the Rimmer family was extremely private and partly because the records are fragmentary or nonexistent, the family history has been shrouded in mystery. According to family legend, Thomas Rimmer, William's father, believed himself to be the younger son of Louis XVI and rightful heir to the throne of France after the death of his older brother in 1789. The story goes that the young dauphin was smuggled out of France to England and placed with a South Lancashire yeo-

For a detailed and fully documented discussion of William Rimmer's life and art, see Jeffrey Weidman, "William Rimmer: Critical Catalogue Raisonné," Ph.D. dissertation, Indiana University, 1982 (published by Ann Arbor: University Microfilms International, 1982), 7 vols. The author is currently working on a monograph on Rimmer to be published by Cambridge University Press in its series Monographs on American Artists.

man family of shoemakers named Rimer. There he was educated with funds from British and Russian friends and received a commission in the British Army. His hopes to assume the French throne were dashed when Louis XVIII, the dead king's brother, became king in 1815. His royal claim now a mark of Cain, he abandoned his commission, married, and went into hiding. In 1818 he emigrated to Nova Scotia, and later, through a series of contacts with Bourbon sympathizers, moved to Boston. By 1827 he and his wife had five children and were living in South Boston. Thomas worked as a laborer, changed the spelling of his name to "Rimmer," and by 1834 had become a bootmaker. He lived the remainder of his life in considerable poverty and died embittered, alcoholic, and insane in 1852.

Nevertheless, during his early years in this country, Thomas Rimmer was able to educate his children in the subjects he had learned, such as music, art, ancient and modern languages, history, and mythology. He also passed on to them a belief in their royal lineage. As his first-born and heir, William Rimmer lived under the psychological, emotional, and social burdens of certain covert expectations that had little possibility of fulfillment. To a certain extent he lived out his father's hopes and frustrations, but the sense of fulfillment he achieved through his art and his family helped him avoid his father's disastrous fate.

Scrapbook material owned by William Rimmer, diary excerpts, other recorded statements, and his own works of art clearly indicate that his supposed royal heritage was a central issue in his life. It provided the source for many of his most powerful and imaginative works of art. Themes of Promethean hubris, expulsion, exile, thwarted ambition, combat, and confrontation recur over and over again in his work, along with lions, gladiators, soldiers, and sentinels. To a certain extent, the royalty issue molded his personality, made him insecure in groups, and caused him to assume what was often perceived as a superior attitude. As it had been for his father, William Rimmer's family life from the 1840's onwards became the center of his social universe, the guardian of his secret, and his buffer against the world.

William Rimmer presented an enigmatic image to the world, an image that has persisted in scholarly writings about him. Some scholars, overwhelmed by the force of Rimmer's personality and the complexities of his origins, have viewed his life as fundamentally isolated and reclusive and his art as enigmatic and often impenetrable. Others have related Rimmer's art and life to Washington Allston's *Belshazzar's Feast*, with Rimmer experiencing like Allston the fate of the isolated artist in America, whose talent and soul withered and died through lack of cultural nourishment.

A deeper and more balanced assessment of William Rimmer's artistic accomplishment and its context has resulted from the last twenty years of scholarship, inspired by the pioneering work of Truman H. Bartlett in the early 1880's and of Lincoln Kirstein in the 1940's. During this period a significant number of important pieces have come to light, among them the marble inkwell *Horse Pulling Stone-Laden Cart* (cat. 1); the drawings *"Oh, for the Horns of the Altar"* (ill. 10) and *Dante and Lion* (cat. 77); and the paintings *Scene from "The Tempest"* (cat. 16), *Scene from "Macbeth"* (cat. 17), *Horses at Fountain* (cat. 19), *Interior / Before the Picture* (cat. 28), *At the Window* (cat. 30), and *Sunset / Contemplation* (cat. 36). With the help of such works we can now see Rimmer as rising above hardship to produce an *oeuvre* in part nurtured by certain European and American works and artistic traditions and in part created as a reaction against those traditions. He enjoyed neither social nor artistic success to any great extent, but his art endures because it touches us with its psychological import, its power, and its universality.

Rimmer's artistic talent emerged early, and by the early 1830's he was capable of producing serious work (see *Seated Man*, cat. 2). Until the 1860's, however, when he assumed the dual career of teacher and artist, he pursued a variety of trades and professions. As a young man he helped support his father's family in the 1830's by setting type, making soap, executing lithographs, and painting signs, portraits, and historical subjects. He received commissions from the Catholic Church and was active in civic and musical events. During this decade a number of his paintings and sculptures were exhibited in Boston. After his marriage in 1840, Rimmer added to his activities that of an itinerant portrait painter in the area south of Boston. In 1845, after it had become clear that he could not make a satisfactory living for his growing family from this work, Rimmer took up shoemaking as his predominant profession.

In the early 1840's, as another means of supplementing his income, Rimmer apprenticed himself to Dr. Abel Washburn Kingman of Brockton for the study of medicine. The innate understanding of expressive anatomy evidenced in his early work was renewed by this study. Essentially self-taught as a doctor, he began his actual practice in the mid-1840's. Although he could be viewed as a typical country doctor, Rimmer favored homeopathic remedies over the use of drugs and was innovative in his water cures for typhoid fever and smallpox. Throughout his later life, Rimmer preferred to be addressed as "Dr. Rimmer," and many of his acquaintances therefore regarded him primarily as a physician and only secondarily as an artist, considering such sculptures as the *St. Stephen* and the *Falling Gladiator* (cat. 5) curios rather than genuine works of art.

The 1840's proved a productive decade for Rimmer, though he was virtually isolated from the cultural and artistic life of Boston and spent most of his creative energies earning a meager living for his family. Besides his own hardships he was burdened with providing for his father, whose health was deteriorating rapidly. Sometime around 1848, Thomas Rimmer was moved from his home in South Boston to a cottage in Concord, where he was discreetly cared for, some of the financial support being provided by Ralph Waldo Emerson. From this time until at least August 1852, when Thomas Rimmer died, William Rimmer's family was in contact with the Emersons and with Bronson Alcott's family. Louisa May Alcott's association with William Rimmer during these years later provided some of the material for the character of Dr. Bhaer in her 1868 novel *Little Women*.

Although never a member of the loosely structured Transcendentalist group *per se*, Rimmer shared with its adherents an unorthodox Christian attitude. It is quite probable that Rimmer's spiritual perspective was formed before his contact with Emerson and Alcott, but their ideas and experiences must have enriched and reinforced his own. The central Transcendentalist tenet of correspondence between the material and the spiritual worlds is found in Rimmer's works, in his writings, and in his fundamental belief in the human body as a microcosm of universal principles. The mystical interpretation of nature as a veil or symbol of the divine is reflected in Rimmer's ideas on painting and in his works of art. Although he often used traditional Christian iconography and scriptural subjects in his works and strongly believed in the miracles of Jesus, he was not bound by denominational prejudices. One could consider him an embodiment of Emerson's concept of "Man Thinking," as expressed in his "American Scholar" address of 1837.

Rimmer's independence from established Christianity extended to the areas of Spiritualism and Freemasonry. His interest in Spiritualism was fostered by psychic experiences, and his association with Freemasonry from 1865 to 1870 informed several of his most compelling works. His now lost sculpture of the *Hawk-Headed Osiris* (1865) may have been partially associated with his membership in the Star of Bethlehem Lodge in Chelsea. Also, his painting *The Master Builder* (cat. 27) from the early 1870's satirizes the folly of trying to interpret externally what should remain an essentially internal Masonic theme. The painting may be related to Rimmer's departure from the lodge at this time.

William Rimmer's spiritual perspective sustained him throughout his father's deterioration, and to a certain extent helped him integrate the meaning of his father's suffering and death into his own life. By the mid-1850's, Rimmer was dealing in a creative and symbolic manner with the psychological impact of his father's life and death. Around this time he began to write a symbolic essay, "Stephen and Phillip," which he worked at on and off for the remainder of his life. This philosophical narrative expressed Rimmer's innermost spiritual questions and convictions about the totality and harmony of man. At the deepest level it represents his relationship with his father, as embodied in two angels, Stephen and Phillip, who symbolize respectively the light and dark aspects of the soul, initially at odds and separated but eventually reconciled and united.

Visual manifestations of this reconciliation of contrasting

elements first appear in Rimmer's paintings from around 1850, *Scene from "The Tempest"* (cat. 16) and *Scene from "Macbeth"* (cat. 17). Although to a large extent Rimmer's work presents us with an iconography of confrontation, supporting his statement that "we live in this world not by let, but by opposition,"[1] one often finds both formal and thematic reconciliations in his works. These two paintings, as well as others like *Juliet and the Nurse* (cat. 20) and *Massacre of the Innocents* (cat. 21), offer some of his most poignant and provocative images.

Although a small number of Rimmer's works are allegorical, such as his large pro-abolitionist drawings from the early 1860's, most of his work in all media is mythic at a most profound level.[2] Rimmer's mythic perspective underlay his artistic and ontological points of view and influenced his thematic and formal choices. It explains his essentially ahistorical approach and his passion for antiquity, the Bible (especially the Book of Job), Dante, Shakespeare, Milton, Bunyan, Michelangelo, Blake, and Beethoven. This same affinity for myth provided him with the creative means to transmute subjects like his supposed royal lineage, his personal suffering, and the nation's anguish from the Civil War into lasting artistic statements.

Rimmer's art can also be seen in terms of a Romantic idealism, as aptly expressed by Washington Allston: "Originality in art is the individualizing the Universal; in other words, the impregnating some general truth with the individual mind."[3] The ability to make a general statement through a single example is seen throughout Rimmer's work and is powerfully expressed in his sculpture. On the one hand, his sculpture adheres to certain neoclassical tenets propagated by Johann Winckelmann (1717–68), such as noble serenity of facial expression and the body's action showing the artist's intention. On the other hand, Rimmer's art is also one of engagement: its powerfully expressive anatomy, three-dimensionality, provocative iconography, and psychological tension demand our attention and elicit our vicarious participation.

Mid-nineteenth-century American academic sculptors like Hiram Powers, William Wetmore Story, and Erastus Dow Palmer interpreted Winckelmann's concept of repose to mean actual physical repose: static, passive, and graceful. Contemporary sculpture presented eternal non-action. Rimmer's finest sculptures, by contrast, are highly energized; what he called "perfect repose"[4] was for him synonymous with latent action. Working within the context of a neoclassical emphasis on eternal, universal values and on placid physiognomy, he further infused his best work with the pathos and expression he so admired in Hellenistic sculpture. Emotional content is expressed through form. Intersecting spirals create a hovering sense of equilibrium between rising and falling forms, as in the *Falling Gladiator* (cat. 5), the *Dying Centaur* (cat. 6), and the *Fighting Lions* (cat. 7). The spirals create a sense of vibrant motion quite different from the static quality of works by Rimmer's contemporaries.

Rimmer's emphasis on the fusion of form and meaning led him to use the classical fragment for its suggestive power. His use of the "partial figure"[5] as a means of expression anticipates Rodin's experiments with fragmentary statues. It is more than coincidental that Rimmer and Rodin, because of their skill in rendering the human body, were accused of having cast a figure from life (Rimmer's *Falling Gladiator* and Rodin's *Age of Bronze*). Both artists transcend the narrative conventions of their era and use the nude to express heroic themes.

A preeminently Romantic element of Rimmer's sculpture, and of much of his other work, is its infusion by "excited

1. Truman H. Bartlett, *The Art Life of William Rimmer: Sculptor, Painter, and Physician* (Boston: James R. Osgood and Company, 1882), p. 104.

2. Today the word "myth" has come to mean untruth or falsehood. Here, however, I use it in the sense of the Greek word "mythos," from which it derives, with its original meaning of a story that was a carrier of truth, a symbolic story possessing living meaning, open-ended and creatively allusive. A mythic perspective implies a universal, comprehensive approach. Myths are atemporal and embrace an urgency about the events to which they relate; they possess power to affect the soul, and their import is numinous.

3. Washington Allston, *Lectures on Art, and Poems* (New York: Baker and Scribner, 1850), p. 172, aphorism 30. Bartlett, *Art Life*, p. 125, wrote of Rimmer that "The great variety with which he treated the same subject suggests the impression that he was not individual, but rather the medium through which the ideal world took form on paper and canvas."

4. The phrase comes from the fourth lecture of Rimmer's second series, given in Providence on Feb. 12, 1872, and reported in "Dr. Rimmer's Lectures," *Providence Daily Journal*, Feb. 14, 1872, p. 1, col. 8. It is also printed in Bartlett, *Art Life*, p. 70.

5. The term is Albert Elsen's in *The Partial Figure in Modern Sculpture from Rodin to 1969* (Baltimore: Baltimore Museum of Art, 1969). Elsen does not mention Rimmer.

spirit."[6] Expressive feeling is a hallmark of his art and of his sculpture in particular. His life-sized busts *Horace Mann* and *Abraham Lincoln* (ills. 3, 4, p. 39) are faithful to their subjects' physiognomy, but the features have been regularized, generalized, and enlivened. More than mere portraits, these busts epitomize Mann's and Lincoln's vigor and genius.

The 1850's were a particularly difficult period for Rimmer. His father's condition deteriorated rapidly until his death in 1852; his wife's health was poor; and five of the eight children born between 1841 and 1857 died in infancy or early childhood. Rimmer's unstable economic situation obliged him to move three times in 1855: first to Lowell for a prospecting venture, then to Chelsea to practice medicine, and finally to East Milton, where he tried to earn a living as a full-time physician. Since most of his patients were granite workers from the nearby Quincy quarries, he had little income and little prospect of earning more.

In 1858, at a time when Rimmer's dire economic situation forced him to begin sculpting in granite, a readily available and inexpensive material, he met Stephen Higginson Perkins (1804–77), who was to play a pivotal role in his artistic career. Related to several prominent Boston families and involved with cultural and civic affairs, Perkins had appraised the contents of Washington Allston's studio after his death in 1843 and had arranged for a number of Allston's engraved drawings to be privately printed at his own expense in 1850.[7] The influence of Allston's work can be seen in some of Rimmer's drawings from the early 1860's, such as *The Struggle Between North and South* (cat. 45) of 1862.

Perkins, who was then living in Milton, recognized Rimmer's artistic genius, befriended him, and became his patron and promoter. He bought *St. Stephen* (ill. 2, p. 38), and shortly after it was displayed in Boston in December 1860 he commissioned the life-sized statue of the *Falling Gladiator*. Referring to Rimmer as "another Michelangelo,"[8] Perkins enthusiastically championed these works both in Boston and in Europe, where he lived between 1862 and 1877 and where he kept the *St. Stephen* and a plaster cast of the *Gladiator*. His letters to Rimmer offer valuable insights into Rimmer's contemplated and finished works during this period.[9]

In his last known letter to Rimmer on December 23, 1868, Perkins wrote:

But this very fact of the bad taste and bad art makes me desirous that you should put at least one work, expressing your ideas of beauty, & dignity & exhibiting your full science, into a permanent form.— . . . The work might not be valued at its true value during my lifetime or yours—but all truly meritorious work, put on record, & kept before the public, is fairly estimated at last.—The work must be in great measure a work of love—to show the next generation, if not this one, where our heads stand.—. . . It does not matter much whether your work is made one year or another—but don't die 'till you've done it, and put all your force and plenty of time and study into it.—

Perkins's prophetic exhortation found immediate manifestation in Rimmer's sculpture of the *Dying Centaur* and later in his *Art Anatomy* drawings (cat. 68–75).

It seems certain that Rimmer's visit to the Sculpture Gallery of the Boston Athenaeum on October 6, 1860, was made possible by Perkins.[10] Normally the Athenaeum's rich and varied collections would have been open only to its members and their guests, except for the annual public exhibitions of paintings begun in 1827.[11] No trips to the Athenaeum before 1860 have been recorded for Rimmer, but it seems likely that Perkins would have made its collections accessible to him. Rimmer

6. The term is David Huntington's in *Art and the Excited Spirit: America in the Romantic Period* (Ann Arbor: University of Michigan Museum of Art, 1972).

7. J. and S. W. Cheney, *Outlines and Sketches by Washington Allston* (Boston: privately printed, 1850).

8. Bartlett, *Art Life*, p. 31. Lincoln Kirstein, in his catalog essay for the 1946–47 Rimmer exhibition at the Whitney Museum of American Art and the Museum of Fine Arts, Boston, writes of Perkins's enthusiasm "over the development of his 'Yankee Michelangelo.'" N.p. (text p. 8).

9. The nineteen letters are in the collection of the Boston Medical Library. Transcriptions of them with short analyses of their contents appear in Weidman, "William Rimmer," 4:1279–1307.

10. Rimmer's visit is documented by a note signed by D. M. Foster, Keeper of the Gallery. This document is in the Boston Medical Library.

11. Founded in 1807 as a proprietary library, the Athenaeum by 1850 owned over 50,000 volumes, with an especially fine collection of anatomy and medical books. By 1860 it also housed a Sculpture Gallery, opened in 1839, with a large collection of plaster casts after antique art and casts of Michelangelo's *Night* and *Day*; the Arundel collection of lithographs of works in the Dresden Gallery, acquired in 1838; the Dowse collection of watercolors after old masters, acquired in 1858; a large selection of paintings by Washington Allston, deposited in 1854; an extensive collection of paintings from all periods by other artists; a collection of over 1,000 plaster casts of antique gems; and a Roman marble copy of the Medici Venus, known to Rimmer since about 1843, when he had seen it at the Harvard Medical School.

certainly knew Perkins's own art collection, and perhaps also the collections of his friends and relatives. During his 1860 visit Rimmer could have seen a full-scale cast of the *Laocoön* group and a cast of the head of *Homer* (still owned by the Athenaeum), as well as Allston's painting of *St. Peter Delivered from Prison* (Museum of Fine Arts, Boston), which was exhibited there from 1860 to 1872. Elements of all these works can be seen in Rimmer's *St. Stephen*, which he began shortly after his visit.

Even if Rimmer had never visited the Athenaeum before his acquaintance with Perkins, he had not been starved for artistic nourishment. From the 1830's onwards, his art shows him to be conversant with the art of antiquity, of the Renaissance, and of his contemporaries. For sculpture Rimmer could have studied plaster casts of Greek and Roman works in the firm of Cicci & Gray on School Street. The Boston Museum and Gallery of Fine Arts, which was actually a theater, contained a large collection of paintings, engravings, marbles, and plaster casts that had been open to the public since 1841. In addition, prints were always available from booksellers and other sources.

The drawing *The Stoning of St. Stephen* (ill. 5, p. 39) shows Rimmer's awareness of prints as early as the mid-1840's. Perhaps intended as an exercise in anatomy related to his medical studies, it nevertheless clearly shows the influence of Italian Renaissance art, especially the prints of Antonio Pollaiuolo. During the same period Rimmer also executed a series of religious paintings for Old St. Mary's in Randolph, Massachusetts, of which the recently discovered *Madonna and Child* (cat. 15) and two paintings known only through Bartlett's biography are all that have been identified.

The first half of the 1860's saw a series of important events that formed Rimmer's reputation as a teacher and artist and to a very large extent propelled him through the rest of his career. The *St. Stephen* and the *Falling Gladiator* marked Rimmer's achievement of artistic maturity and opened the period during which he would produce the vast majority of his works and establish a reputation as a teacher. With the help of friends such as Perkins, James Elliot Cabot, and William R. Ware, Rimmer became involved with the artistic and intellectual life of Boston. By early 1862 he had joined the prestigious Boston

Art Club and was teaching in the Studio Building. Rimmer's reputation for astounding audiences with his lectures on artistic anatomy led to his being invited to give a series of ten talks for the Lowell Institute in Boston, beginning in October 1863. The success of the first series prompted Rimmer to move from East Milton to Chelsea and to relinquish his medical practice for a full-time teaching and artistic career. The male students who attended these lectures formed a private art school in Boston and invited Rimmer to serve as its director. His lectures were so popular that he was asked to return to the Lowell Institute in the spring of 1864 to repeat the first series.

Of all the illustrious and influential persons who supported Rimmer in this private school, perhaps the most significant in terms of Rimmer's public image was William Morris Hunt (1824–79), a leading artist and teacher in Boston. During the 1860's and 1870's, Hunt and Rimmer were both popular teachers and indeed were often compared. Rimmer's pedagogical reputation was certainly as deserved as Hunt's, but Hunt, coming from a prestigious and wealthy family, was better adapted to Boston's social world. Although their artistic and pedagogical approaches differed and they were perceived to be at odds, Hunt and Rimmer admired one another. In the public's eye Rimmer stood for probity of line, Hunt for atmospheric color and form. Yet they sent students to each other, and in 1878 Hunt sought and received Rimmer's help in composing his designs for the Albany State Capitol murals commission. Hunt died just after Rimmer in 1879; they were both honored in 1880 by exhibitions held at the recently founded Museum of Fine Arts, the first and second such exhibitions respectively.

During 1864 and 1865 Rimmer's renown was substantially increased by a series of publications and events. In 1864, soon after a number of Boston newspapers had praised his teaching, Rimmer's primer on drawing, *Elements of Design*, was published, making it possible to spread his pedagogical reputation beyond Boston. Around the same time, his supporters published a pamphlet entitled *Opinions of Some Distinguished Artists and Connoisseurs in Reference to Dr. Rimmer's Works*, which reprinted the accolades accorded the *St. Stephen* and the *Falling Gladiator* by European critics and artists and by such illustrious American expatriate sculptors as Story and

Powers. These two sculptures received additional praise from the influential art critic James Jackson Jarves in his book *The Art-Idea*, published soon afterward.

A number of the extracts in the *Opinions* pamphlet actually came from Perkins's letters to Rimmer. Although he lived in Florence, Perkins continued to exert an influence on Rimmer's career in Boston. One result was Rimmer's first public commission, the granite statue of *Alexander Hamilton* (frontispiece) on Commonwealth Avenue, given to the city by Thomas Lee. The statue was unveiled on August 25, 1865, just before Rimmer began a series of lectures at Harvard University.

Although most twentieth-century critics have praised Rimmer's *Hamilton*, nineteenth-century critics generally failed to appreciate its formal and symbolic qualities. The statue is essentially an idealized representation of the man, with minimal concessions to portraiture in the details of hair and clothing. The drapery suggests a toga, a fitting classical allusion for the Federalist Hamilton. The powerfully suggestive configuration of head, drapery, and mass foreshadows Rodin's *Balzac* of 1897, a conceptual connection first noted in 1916.[12] The unfavorable reaction to the *Hamilton*, among other considerations, encouraged Rimmer to look toward New York as a more favorable artistic climate. He delivered a successful lecture at the National Academy of Design in January of 1866, and soon afterward accepted an offer to become Director of the School of Design for Women at Cooper Union for the Advancement of Science and Art. During the four years he held the post, from 1866 to 1870, Rimmer retained his newly acquired home in Chelsea and spent his summers in New England. Not everyone at Cooper Union approved of his pedagogical program, which drew increasing internal criticism; and when he returned in the fall of 1870 to find his duties restricted, he resigned his post. Nevertheless, Rimmer's years in New York were fruitful: not only was he artistically productive, but he achieved the social acceptance denied him in Boston. He called the four years he spent in New York the happiest of his life.[13]

Returning to Boston, Rimmer reestablished his teaching career. As in the 1860's, his lectures on artistic anatomy provided his main source of income until his death in 1879. His study of medicine and anatomy during the 1840's and his practice of medicine until the early 1860's are intimately associated with the content and method of his teaching. Our knowledge of Rimmer's teaching comes from a variety of sources, both written and visual, produced by Rimmer and his students. These include his own *Elements of Design* (1864) and *Art Anatomy* (1877); material by and about Rimmer from the Cooper Union years; published reports of his second and third series of lectures, given in Providence during 1872 and 1873; material in Bartlett's *Art Life* (1882); and sketchbooks of his students, among them Hammatt Billings and Daniel Chester French.

Rimmer's teaching method was a systematization of the process of self-study he had himself gone through for the practice of medicine and for the creation of his own works, especially his life-sized *Falling Gladiator* (cat. 5) of 1861. Rimmer received his anatomical knowledge from books and from observation, from dissection and from study of the musculature of a contemporary gymnast, Henry K. Bushnell. His knowledge of ancient sculpture, through plaster casts, prints, and an occasional marble, contributed to the formation of his aesthetic and to his teaching method.

In his lectures Rimmer used a human skeleton, life-sized colored charts of the human body, a cast of Houdon's *Écorché*, and, during the 1860's, his own *Falling Gladiator* and *Hawk-Headed Osiris*. Most of all he relied on a large blackboard and a piece of chalk. Equipped with these simple items, Rimmer first analyzed the separate parts of the body and their functions and then presented their synthesis in complete figures and compositions. He also discussed the functions of the human mind as manifested through expression, and offered ethnological and typological comparisons.

Male and female students copied individual drawings into their sketchbooks. Rimmer would criticize these separately, or a student would draw on the blackboard and Rimmer would discuss the student's drawing for the benefit of the entire group. Eventually, advanced students would work from a nude model.

12. A. J. Philpott, "Little Appreciated Genius: Exhibition of Paintings, Sculptures and Other Works by Dr. William Rimmer," *The Boston Globe*, Feb. 20, 1916, p. 21.
13. Bartlett, *Art Life*, p. 59.

Lecturing was difficult for Rimmer, but he sometimes became so engrossed in drawing that he would cover the blackboard with forms. Rimmer identified completely with the creative process; indeed, to some students he seemed more concerned with awakening their creativity than with leading them through the intricacies of anatomical and artistic study. Rimmer's method was designed for the talented person who could quickly grasp the analysis of the parts as well as their synthesis. He directly affected many artists through his teaching, most notably French, Hunt, John La Farge, Anne Whitney, Frederick Vinton, and Frank Benson.

Rimmer's concept of anatomy embraced his most fundamental thoughts on man and his relationship to the cosmos. From his early *Seated Man* (cat. 2) to the *Art Anatomy* drawings some 45 years later, Rimmer used the human body to express his heroic conception of man. This approach renders intelligible his repeated remark that "Anatomy is the only subject."[14] Rimmer abhorred the study of what he called "morbid anatomy,"[15] i.e., of the muscles in isolation, and also disliked structural anatomy, or "anatomy in the abstract"[16] without reference to its connection with physiology, pathology, or the practice of medicine or surgery. He believed that only the most advanced art students should study dissection lest their creativity become mired in scientific fact.

As early as the late 1840's, Rimmer's attitude toward anatomy can be seen in a marginal drawing of a standing nude male (cat. 41) in his copy of Cruveilhier's *Anatomy of the Human Body*. As he matured he further elaborated, refined, and systematized his thoughts on the subject. His *Elements of Design* (1864) emphasizes learning to draw the human figure not by copying artists but by studying the possibilities inherent in human limbs in action. This emphasis, as well as the high ratio of plates to text, distinguishes Rimmer's book from many previous and contemporary art instruction books in America.

Art Anatomy (1877) contains the fullest development of Rimmer's pedagogical approach. Although Rimmer himself did not regard it as his final statement on the subject,[17] its illustrations fully display the possibilities inherent in his admonition to "make no display of technical anatomy. A work of art should be something more than the solution of a problem in

science."[18] *Art Anatomy* demands the full attention and concentration of the intermediate or advanced student. It is a textbook that is also a fully realized work of art, combining approximately 850 separate images on 81 large, elaborate sheets with explanatory text, suppositional statements, and questions directed to the student.

Art Anatomy may have been initially conceived as a reply to Hunt's *Talks on Art*, published in 1875, but Rimmer's book is both more focused and more elaborate. Rimmer executed the drawings during the summer of 1876, mainly in Union, New Hampshire. They are exquisitely drawn in fine, hard, gray pencil; some are in outline, others tonal. The drawings demonstrate Rimmer's synthesis of many authorities on medicine, human and comparative anatomy, physiognomy, phrenology, and ethnology, including Galen, Vesalius, Albinus, Lavater, and contemporaries such as Jeffries Wyman and Louis Agassiz. They also reveal his study of the crania and other collections of the Warren Museum of Natural History in Boston and his awareness of comparative studies by Thomas Huxley and Charles Darwin. Rimmer's open-mindedness, combined with his clinical experience and close study of classical sculpture, allowed him to recognize the creative aspects of physiognomy and of phrenology while rejecting the unscientific tenets of both.

Two of the most remarkable aspects about the *Art Anatomy* drawings are their rapidity of execution and the apparent lack of preliminary sketches. Each of the 81 sheets appears to have been executed without hesitation or revision. Rimmer rarely relied on preliminary sketches for his work. In fact, no preparatory drawings for Rimmer's surviving sculpture are known, and only a very few exist for his paintings.

Although a number of Rimmer's drawings appear to have come from sketchbooks, only one such book survives, the so-called Bates Sketchbook at the Boston Medical Library. Its twelve drawings are closer to fully developed compositions than to tentative ideas. Rimmer's earliest drawings were done

14. *Ibid.*, p. 86.   15. *Ibid.*, p. 135.
16. *Ibid.*, p. 64.   17. *Ibid.*, p. 86.
18. On drawing (sheet) 12 of Part II, *Art Anatomy*, "The Neck Muscles." The second sentence is also printed in Bartlett, *Art Life*, p. 104.

in the 1820's, and drawings constitute the majority of his work. Most are in pencil, both outline and tonal; some are in sepia and sanguine. One watercolor survives.

From the printing techniques available to Rimmer, he chose lithography and drypoint. His initial lithographic work was done for Thomas Moore's firm in the late 1830's, and most of his lithographs were done between then and the mid-1840's. The subtle modulations of light and shade that are possible in this medium are echoed in his later drawings. Rimmer's work in drypoint, with its velvety blurs of ink, allowed him to combine the freedom and rapidity of drawing with the rich atmospheric effects of lithography. The majority of his drypoint prints are from the mid-1860's and may have been initiated by his association with Cooper Union.

During most of his life, Rimmer worked with prodigious speed and under difficult conditions. This is particularly true of his sculptures, such as *St. Stephen*, completed in four weeks in his woodhouse; *Falling Gladiator*, completed in four months in an unheated, poorly lit basement; the model for *Hawk-Headed Osiris*, completed in seven days; and the model for *Alexander Hamilton*, completed in eleven days in an unheated church. For his sculptures, except for the finished statue of *Hamilton*, Rimmer did all the work. His early works were cut in stone, but even when working in clay he preferred to carve rather than to model. For this reason Rimmer's contemporaries associated him with Michelangelo and with Neoplatonic philosophy, which saw sculpture as the act of freeing form from mass.

Rimmer's rapid execution can be partially explained by the relatively little time he had for his art. Before the early 1860's art was a sporadic avocation for him, and later the act of creation was subordinated to his teaching. Rimmer was never able to earn a living from his art works alone. Indeed, although the quality of his art was in no way diminished by its rapid execution, his contemporaries tended to dismiss work executed with apparent ease. This was especially true of his sculptures. Rimmer's working method was deemed incommensurate with the gravity of the commission; speed was perceived as both an aesthetic and a moral flaw.

The key to understanding Rimmer's technique in all media is to recognize his ability to form an image in his mind and rework it there until conditions arose whereby he could commit it to material form (e.g., the commissions for the *Gladiator* and for the *Art Anatomy* drawings). Rimmer apparently used a living model only once, for the human body of his *Hawk-Headed Osiris*.

Rimmer's choice of material in sculpture seems to have been primarily defined by what was readily available and thus economical. When given a choice of stone, he preferred granite for its color, pattern, texture, and durability. In the gypsum *Seated Man* (cat. 2) and the granite *St. Stephen* (ill. 2) the choice of materials also has a symbolic aspect. He would work in marble if the stone were available or if the terms of the commission specified that material. There is no indication that he planned to have any of his work cast in bronze.

Rimmer's ignorance of technique contributed considerably to his problems. The *Falling Gladiator* (cat. 5) was done in clay in his unheated basement during the winter. Lacking an armature, the clay froze and broke apart. After partially rebuilding the piece, Rimmer had it cast in plaster and then finished it in this material. Several years later he experienced similar problems with the *Hamilton* model, but through sheer determination he was able to complete the commission.

It is possible to gain some understanding of Rimmer's erratic attention to technique by seeing it in the context of his mythic approach. He was consumed by a passion to express principles of great magnitude, and in his haste he often neglected technical details. It is also true that because his commissions brought him relatively little income, he felt he had to work quickly.

Technical ignorance also affected his paintings, the most adverse result being the darkening of bitumen and resulting surface deterioration. Although Rimmer exhibited very few paintings and was not generally known by his contemporaries as a painter, his work in this medium constitutes approximately one-quarter of his *oeuvre*. He had relatively little time to spare for this activity, but hoped one day to "revel in paint."[19] Never enjoying the "luxuries of a well-appointed studio,"[20] Rimmer

19. Bartlett, *Art Life*, p. 126.   20. *Ibid.*

painted wherever he could, "on the floor in the sitting room, in the hall-way, on the stairs, or in the attic."[21] His paintings tend to be small in size, but many are of compelling interest.

That Rimmer intended his paintings to stir the imagination is suggested by his images and by his statement that "there should be an element of mystery in every picture."[22] His work is characterized by delicate colors and a subtle, atmospheric quality created by painting very thinly. The ethereal quality is sometimes heightened by the absence of a middle ground in his compositions, which gives them a compressed, two-dimensional, dreamlike effect. Rimmer's writings on color indicate that this effect was intended to express symbolic themes: "Above all, remember atmosphere, that impalpable something which we feel but do not see, which softens every defect, and throws over everything a thin, transparent veil."[23]

This kind of atmosphere is most apparent in Rimmer's paintings from the 1870's, beginning, for example, with *Interior/Before the Picture* (cat. 28) and *Flight and Pursuit* (cat. 29) of 1872. It increases through the decade and is pronounced in a work such as *The Shepherd* (cat. 37) of 1877. The shadowy quality of many of Rimmer's paintings creates a mysterious ambience, which has unintentionally been accentuated by the darkening of bitumen: e.g., *Horses at Fountain* (cat. 19), *At the Window* (cat. 30), and *Picture Buyers* (cat. 33).

Rimmer considered color, which he believed could by itself express the underlying meaning of an image, to be independent of form; he looked on color as a "garment" that could envelop his image and "assist in expressing the sentiment of the subject."[24] Even in his most somber color schemes one can usually find a touch of English red vermilion to ornament the image. These coloristic qualities, often combined with barely visible brush strokes and precise, linear forms, suggest that Rimmer was also influenced by academic painting, such as the work of Gérôme, to whose work he referred both in his lectures and in his paintings. Whatever his sources may have been, his use of color contributes to the overall impact of his images and is a recognizable stylistic feature of his work.

Approximately eight months after *Art Anatomy* was published in September 1877, Rimmer began teaching at the newly founded School of the Museum of Fine Arts in Boston. His classes were well attended, but as at Cooper Union ten years earlier, he encountered difficulties with school administrators over curriculum. The strain seems to have affected both his health and his artistic output; the number of works done during 1877–79 is small. Another contributing factor was the disappointingly slow sales of *Art Anatomy*, despite its favorable critical reception.

Ill as he was, in 1878 Rimmer abandoned his essentially apolitical stance to produce some visual propaganda for workers involved in a labor crisis in Fall River. *The Poor Man Has Nothing to Lose* (cat. 85) shows Rimmer as a kind of Christian Socialist in the utopian tradition of Charles Fournier. It also suggests that any inherited aristocratic propensities had been democratized, and displays his belief in the Emersonian qualities of self-reliance and nonconformity. Rimmer's social beliefs are further exemplified by his pro-abolitionist drawings of the early 1860's and in the passionate statements quoted by Truman Bartlett. A number of his published poems, such as "Autumn" (1850) and "The Love Chant: A Satire" (1874), also clearly display his bent for social criticism.[25]

In the spring of 1879 Rimmer suffered a mental and physical collapse that forced him to abandon his duties at the Museum School about two months before the end of the term. Resting at the home of his daughter Adeline and her husband, George Durham, in South Milford, he kept mentally active by planning the fall's teaching. However, his health worsened and he turned once more to myth, spending his last days reading his manuscript of "Stephen and Phillip." Rimmer's death on August 20 was noted in several obituaries. He was buried in the Milton Cemetery.

21. *Ibid.*, p. 128. This was told to Bartlett by a member of the Rimmer family.

22. Rimmer's observation was reported in "Dr. Rimmer's Twelvth [sic] Lecture," *Providence Daily Journal*, Mar. 19, 1873, p. 2, col. 8.

23. Bartlett, *Art Life*, p. 147.

24. *Ibid.*

25. These poems are contained in the Rimmer Album at the Boston Medical Library along with other poems and drawings. Transcriptions and discussions of Rimmer's poetry in this album appear in Weidman, "William Rimmer," 4:1260–78.

Three weeks after Rimmer's death, his 29-year-old former pupil Daniel Chester French summed up his opinion of his teacher, and perhaps also his contemporaries' assessment of Rimmer's life and art: "The poor long-suffering doctor! His was an unhappy and unsuccessful life. He just missed being great."[26] Yet some 37 years later, in 1916, French wrote of *St. Stephen* (ill. 2), the *Falling Gladiator* (cat. 5), the *Dying Centaur* (cat. 6), and the *Fighting Lions* (cat. 7): "When we consider the period at which these works were executed we cannot fail to be impressed with the independence and originality of the mind that conceived them. They are so opposed to all the sculpture that was being done at the time. These works are real sculpture and exhibit knowledge and feeling and sculpturesque qualities that are rare in any age."[27]

When one objectively considers William Rimmer's character, his background, his education and training, and the other external and internal contingencies that affected his life, the man and his work must be considered astonishing phenomena. The number of his works was not especially large (approximately 600: 45 sculptures, 160 paintings, and nearly 400 drawings), but the quality of those that survive is high. When we reflect also that fewer than one-quarter of his works were commissioned, and that even for these the payment was not great, we can only marvel at his output.

Although struggle against fate is a leitmotif of Rimmer's art, his ability to maintain a certain detachment allowed him to transcend personal suffering through creativity. It was Rimmer's own genius that enabled him to take the raw material of personal experience and fashion it into statements of universal import.

26. French's comments are contained in his letter of September 10, 1870, to Mrs. Thomas Ball, the sculptor's wife, who was then living in Italy. It is quoted by Lincoln Kirstein in his catalog essay.
27. French's comments are contained in his letter of Feb. 14, 1916, to "The Art Editor" of the *Boston Transcript*, and were elicited by the imminent Rimmer exhibition at the Museum of Fine Arts.

WILLIAM RIMMER: THE ARTIST AS TEACHER

Neil Harris

William Rimmer did not fit easily into the American scene. And it is not immediately apparent how his career can be made to represent national trends or achievements. Artists, to be sure, rarely exemplify average conditions. The nature of their work and the source of their ambitions put them outside the mainstream, if not in outright opposition to it.

Rimmer, however, stands out even among his fellow artists. Mysterious ancestry, personal tragedies, medical training, limited output, and a baffling obscurity combine to make his life something of an unusual aside, a quixotic pause in the ongoing story of American art. This catalog and this exhibition, which reestablish the details of his career and reconsider the quality of his artistry, represent one effort at reclamation. But there are also aspects to Rimmer's life and contemporary reputation that make suggestive links to his generation. They demonstrate that even so exotic a type did not fully escape the flavor of his culture.

Rimmer abundantly fulfilled a series of assumptions about the artist life that were well established in mid-century America. There was, for example, his lack of formal training. During his evolution from the simplest branches of commercial art up through the higher aspirations of allegory and history, Rimmer taught himself. He was not exceptional. By 1850 many an American artist had proudly proclaimed himself to be a child of nature, exempt from the vices accompanying years of professional study. Lengthy itinerary as a face painter or a sign painter had frequently preceded the glories of history painting or heroic sculpture. Benjamin West, the Pennsylvania lad who

would become a favorite of George III, was the most striking example, but many others were forced to learn on the road, lucky to find a few original works of art to copy, some books, and primitive art supplies. Thomas Cole wandered through Ohio and Pennsylvania painting scenery, signs, and occasional faces while developing his landscape art. Chester Harding, later a prominent Boston portraitist, toured as a sign painter, commissioning his portrait by more practiced hands simply to learn how it was done. Others, if they were lucky, attached themselves to the studio of an older artist and learned by imitation—if they had enough time to spare.

Rimmer exemplified another artistic virtue: he was poor, at times desperately poor, despite the additional income his medical work brought in. The poverty theme was raised constantly in artists' memoirs, letters, and biographical portraits. As some saw it in mid-century America, the artist's life represented an antidote to the prevailing materialism of the time. By choice or by unhappy necessity, it was hard to imagine a well-paid artist. Except for a fortunate few born to wealth or skillful in obtaining private patronage, painters, sculptors, lithographers, and engravers all scrambled to make a living. Continued exposure to luxury—in the homes of wealthy clients, for example—sometimes embittered those who lived by the brush or the chisel.

Finally, Rimmer epitomized another classic theme. To friends and admirers he seemed isolated, unappreciated, doomed to intellectual and aesthetic as well as financial disappointment. Rimmer, wrote his nineteenth-century biographer,

Truman H. Bartlett, "lived and studied in worse than solitude, for he constantly felt the burden of an unsympathetic world. He shunned men, and knew neither art nor artists." A "sensitive understanding and positive love" of sculpture, insisted Bartlett, himself a sculptor, "does not yet exist."[1] Although Rimmer's personal qualities heightened his sense of isolation, many nineteenth-century American artists and critics complained of living at a time and place where art commanded little respect. Copley had sounded the theme in the eighteenth century, and Washington Allston's followers expanded on it during the next generation.[2] Many an émigré repeated the charge in the decades after Rimmer's death: Americans paid too little attention to their serious artists, forcing them to find hospitality elsewhere.

But these broad, rather general ties between Rimmer and attitudes to the art life in America take no account of major changes in professional practice, and understate the expanding opportunities available to artists seeking larger reputations. This expansion took place within Rimmer's lifetime; some of the attention he gained rested on the increasing elaboration of the American art world and the routinization of professional training and evaluation. Despite his personal obscurity, poverty, and lack of certification, Rimmer benefited from the basic institutional changes that were taking place around him.

There was, for example, his career as teacher and lecturer. It was the invitation to offer a lecture series for the Lowell Institute that first brought Rimmer to the notice of a wider audience, and he received this invitation in part because he had already begun to do some teaching in Boston. His studio occupied space in the Studio Building at the corner of Tremont and Bromfield Streets, the city's most prominent (and concentrated) work setting for artists. By the Civil War era studio buildings in larger cities had become arenas for the exercising of artists' social and aesthetic ambitions.[3] Here artists not only could get their work done but could put themselves on display, as often as not against a background of exotic props gathered in travel abroad. Although Rimmer seemed to scorn the social graces and did not travel in Europe, he gained from the new density of the artist community. His early lectures, in room 55 of the Studio Building, were attended (according to his biog-

rapher, Bartlett) by "old and young of all classes and both sexes,—by artists who wished to learn, by literary people who came to enjoy an intellectual feast, and by physicians. . . . It was the first living element in art instruction Boston had ever possessed."[4] Rimmer was a performer, helped by the presence of a new, heterogeneous audience.

The growing interest in lectures and self-improvement suggests another aspect of the increasingly elaborated American art world: its involvement with specialized education. Art instruction was not simply a matter of training professional artists, but also involved creating classes for lay people. Rimmer's impressive series of lecture engagements, spanning two decades, suggests how deeply this need was felt. The Lowell presentations, which succeeded his Studio Building talks, drew large crowds, and Rimmer thereupon produced an extra afternoon series for ladies. Some Bostonians tried to get him a permanent appointment at the Lowell Institute; others sought to create a new art school under his direction. His sponsors included some of the city's great names—Holmes, Shaw, Ward, Brimmer, Cabot, and Perkins. And such a school did open. Rimmer's move to New York City in the fall of 1866 also built on his lecturing success. Earlier that year Peter Cooper had been so impressed that he persuaded Cooper Union to invite him for lectures, and there followed several years of directing that institution's School of Design for Women.

1. Truman H. Bartlett, *The Art Life of William Rimmer: Sculptor, Painter, and Physician* (Boston and New York: Houghton Mifflin, 1890) p. 38. The book was originally published in 1882.
2. Rimmer was "out of his element in America, and might as well have produced his work in the wilds of Africa," Bartlett wrote in the *Art Life*, p. 49, after a lengthy discussion of his handicaps. Artists' recollections and biographies emphasize the isolation theme. For one example among many, see William Wetmore Story's comment to James Lowell in 1885: "Allston starved spiritually in Cambridgeport—he fed upon himself. There was nothing congenial without & he introverted all his powers & drained his memory dry. His work grew thinner & vaguer every day & in his old age he ruined his great picture." As quoted in William H. Gerdts and Theodore E. Stebbins, Jr., "A Man of Genius": The Art of Washington Allston (1779–1843) (Boston: Museum of Fine Arts, 1979).
3. For more on the art life in Boston in the nineteenth century, see Carol Troyen, *The Boston Tradition: American Paintings from the Museum of Fine Arts, Boston* (New York: American Federation of Arts, 1980). The Studio Building was erected in 1862. For more on studio buildings and artistic centralization, see Neil Harris, *The Artist in American Society: The Formative Years* (New York: Braziller, 1966), pp. 267–72.
4. Bartlett, *Art Life of William Rimmer*, p. 39.

The Lowell Institute lectures, a series of lecture visits to Providence (covered and summarized by newspaper reporters), and the Cooper Union program all stimulated and drew on a larger movement in the 1860's and 1870's, including the growth of proprietary and normal schools for drawing.[5] The object was to raise the level of American design. Americans visiting Europe found its systems of art education impressive. They saw the ways in which official support by the German, French, Austrian, and British governments improved industrial design, and they saw that good designers aided industrial capacity by encouraging exports. In 1864 the city of Boston made drawing instruction compulsory in all common schools. In 1870 the Boston School Committee appointed a well-known British educator, Walter Smith, as Director of Drawing for the Boston Schools, and Smith then became State Director of Art Education. In 1873 the Massachusetts State Normal Art School was established in Boston to train drawing teachers. Within a decade or so dozens of American cities would make drawing a compulsory school subject. By the end of the 1880's more than thirty schools of design were functioning in the United States, and a number of important museums had been founded; both developments resulted partly from a desire to raise the standards of applied art in America and so improve national taste. And just over the horizon were important new textbooks and curricula developed by progressive educators, who related art instruction to the development of many levels of personal skill.

Education in the so-called fine arts was also expanding.[6] Schools attached to the National Academy of Design in New York and the Pennsylvania Academy of Fine Arts had been created much earlier in the century. Cooper Union, with broad social goals, was established in 1857, the Washington University School of Fine Arts in St. Louis in 1879, the Corcoran School of Art in Washington one year later, and the Rhode Island School of Design in 1877. Important art schools were also part of The Art Institute of Chicago, the Cincinnati Art Museum, and Yale University. During the late nineteenth century a number of American artists gained reputations that depended in large part on their teaching. They included Eugene Neuhaus of the California School of Design in San Francisco;

John H. Vanderpoel of The Art Institute of Chicago and the People's University in St. Louis; Frank A. Parsons, director of the New York School of Fine and Applied Art; Frank Duveneck, who taught in both Munich and Cincinnati; William Merritt Chase, like Duveneck a distinguished artist but a remarkable teacher at both the Art Students' League in New York City and his school near Southampton, on Long Island; Eric Papé, an illustrator who set up a school in Boston in the 1890's; and Paul Cornoyer, Kenneth Hayes-Miller, Thomas Anschutz, and Thomas Eakins of the Pennsylvania Academy of Fine Arts. To some extent Rimmer anticipated this pattern. The real growth in faculty and enrollments occurred after his death. But he had important professional pupils, and many attending his classes were caught up in the urge to learn more about the artist's techniques.

Rimmer's success as an artist-pedagogue rested less on his publishing than on his lecture-demonstrations. Authoring a book had long been one way to fame. Although few artists, in England or America, attained the influence Sir Joshua Reynolds gained with his *Discourses*, a number of Americans, including Horatio Greenough and Washington Allston, published lectures on art, and dozens of others, including John G. Chapman, put out drawing manuals.[7] Rimmer's manual, which appeared in 1864, was not particularly original. His *Art*

5. There is need for further writing on the history of American art education. Some useful works are Frederick M. Logan, *Growth of Art in American Schools* (New York: Harper, 1955), Stuart Macdonald, *The History and Philosophy of Art Education* (New York: American Elsevier, 1970), and Frederick C. Moffatt, *Arthur Wesley Dow (1857–1922)* (Washington: Smithsonian Institution Press, 1977).

6. Some sense of the variety of schools and their faculties can be culled from the *American Art Annual*, which began to appear in 1903. In addition to news of museums, art sales and auctions, obituaries, and biographical indices, the *Annual* frequently had listings and reports on art schools. Sometimes founding dates would be included; for one list see Florence N. Levy, ed., *American Art Annual*, 9 (1911): 293–306. By the 1880's articles on art schools in various cities had begun to appear in magazines. We now have histories of the major schools, as well as biographical and monographic studies of significant artist-teachers like Chase, Eakins, and Duveneck.

7. Some sense of the variety of this literature can be gained by glancing through Robert Goldwater and Marco Treves, eds., *Artists on Art: From the XIV to the XX Century* (New York: Pantheon, 1945, 1947). See also William H. Gerdts, "The American 'Discourses': A Survey of Lectures and Writings on American Art, 1770–1858," *American Art Journal*, 15.3 (Summer 1983): 61–79.

Anatomy of 1877 was far more striking, thanks to its use of his own illustrations. But despite its publishers' belief that it did more for Rimmer's reputation than any of his "works of art,"[8] it came out in a disappointingly small edition and only two years before Rimmer's death.

It was as a platform performer, then, that Rimmer had his most notable pedagogical impact. Here there were few American precedents for him to learn from. As he spoke Rimmer drew in chalk on a blackboard, not merely illustrating or exemplifying his comments on anatomy but creating compositions that were extraordinary in themselves. His experience as a physician added to his persuasiveness as a commentator on human anatomy. Students found the oral explanations pungent and exhaustive, and the drawing skills masterly. Those in class were expected to copy the drawings, absorb Rimmer's comments, proceed themselves to sketch on the blackboard, and accept further criticism. The method demanded quickness, a thick skin, and a good memory.

But it was difficult to reduce Rimmer's technique to a formula. Truman Bartlett stressed its inspirational nature: "Once touched by the charm of expressing his long-accumulating knowledge, Dr. Rimmer became inspired; and the study of anatomical forms, which had hitherto been dry and irksome, became, under his lucid descriptions, electric presence, and skillful hand, an enchanting pursuit."[9]

Not all students responded as favorably. Although most admired Rimmer's energy, intensity, and magnetism, they disagreed about his effectiveness as a teacher. "The man claimed and received all my attention," one former student recalled, adding that he was never able to follow the figures that Rimmer drew on the blackboard; "far greater than the task that occupied him," Rimmer belonged not in a classroom but in a studio, where he would be free to explore his creative visions. Another student agreed that Rimmer inspired his audiences, but added "it did not last." Although one student asserted that "his teaching excited me as nothing of the sort that had ever been done before," another felt that Rimmer "lacked taste, and could not always distinguish between good and bad." Described variously as "stubborn and unmanageable," "too much of a *doctrinaire*," and "a guide, not a teacher," Rimmer was also praised as a "romancer, who, out of an unknown world, strung an endless procession of noble forms. His nature was very refined, but impracticable and queer."[10]

Rimmer's students, like some of his critics, thus expressed their ambivalence about his true qualities. Brilliance and commitment were abundantly present in this charismatic personality, but something was missing. The lectures dazzled and entertained, but did not always instruct. Rimmer's educational career had sharp ups and downs. Great successes preceded disappointing failures, and the security and control that he longed for were invariably withdrawn.

A sense of unfulfilled promise, missed opportunities, and stunted professional development shadowed Rimmer for the last two decades of his life. Some were not certain about the responsibility. Was it Rimmer's, or New England's? Was the artist simply too refined, too idealistic? Or was he actually arrogant and proud, too emotionally crippled to handle social relationships? Rimmer, one of his colleagues announced hopefully, "is to be remembered for what he was, and what he did; not for what he was not, or what he did not do."[11] However reasonable the thought, it was not prophetic. Rimmer was mourned for his failures even more than he was admired for his successes. His blighted career could be seen either as the inevitable result of personal problems, or as the product of a culture that failed to recognize genius. Either way it exemplified the national tragedy of the American artist, as romantics worked and reworked the theme.

There was, to be sure, a brighter side to the New England art world, as exemplified by an artist who was almost a precise contemporary of Rimmer's; indeed, they died the same year. Bostonians liked to couple their names and conjure up a rivalry; Truman Bartlett's biography returned to the relationship again and again. Rimmer's alter ego was the painter, patron, and collector William Morris Hunt. Born eight years after Rimmer, the son of a judge and Congressman, Hunt spent his

8. From the unpaginated "Publisher's Note," William Rimmer, *Art Anatomy* (Boston and New York: Houghton Mifflin, 1877, 1905).

9. Bartlett, *Art Life of William Rimmer*, p. 41.

10. These comments were grouped by Bartlett in his Supplement to the *Art Life*, pp. 133–47. 11. *Ibid.*, p. 141.

early years in Europe as a student of Thomas Couture and Jean-François Millet. While Rimmer lived "in the withering sterility of a New-England village," studying in "worse than solitude," feeling the "burden of an unsympathetic world," as Bartlett put it, Hunt feasted on European art, drinking "at every refreshing, golden source" and affected by "every glorious, reviving art-influence."[12] On returning to Boston Hunt helped popularize the new Barbizon school, befriended young artists, and organized receptions and salons in his studio. His clients bore some of the greatest names of the region: Bacon, Saltonstall, Adams, Loring, Hoar, Paine, and Winthrop. Describing Hunt as amiable, earnest, sympathetic, and above all generous, his biographer showed him surrounded by friends admiring "his brilliant conversational powers, his originality of thought and action, and his rare wit."[13] So many demands were made on Hunt's time that many of his portraits went unfinished.

If Rimmer represented the dark side of New England's art tradition, Hunt was its sunny side. But despite the powerful contrasts, two parallels are arresting. First of all, like Rimmer, Hunt was intensely interested in pedagogy. Concerned about instructional opportunities for young artists, he toyed with the idea of opening an art school with his brother Richard; he even contacted Rimmer about the possibility of a joint program. Though he never did open a school, Hunt always had a large number of pupils.

Second, again like Rimmer, Hunt enjoyed the services of a near-contemporary biographer. Indeed, the two biographies bore similar titles. Helen M. Knowlton published the *Art Life of William Morris Hunt* in 1899, twenty years after Hunt's death and seventeen years after Truman Bartlett's *Art Life of William Rimmer*. But in this competition at least, Rimmer gained the advantage, for Bartlett's book is a remarkable and fascinating enterprise.[14]

It was not uncommon for friends or admirers of nineteenth-century American artists to gather their letters, observations and writings together and publish them along with a brief biography. Thus John Galt's romanticized *Life, Studies, and Works of Benjamin West* appeared in 1820, the year of West's death; and the Reverend Louis Noble's life of Thomas Cole (1853) would dominate accounts of that painter for almost one hun-

dred years. Many decades later the sculptor William Wetmore Story benefited from the attentions of Henry James; Washington Allston's correspondence was edited for publication by the painter Jared B. Flagg; and George Inness, Asher B. Durand, G. P. A. Healy, Seth Cheney, and Horatio Greenough were among the many artists whose writings and observations were made available to the public by the sympathetic efforts of widows, siblings, children, and grandchildren. These texts are invaluable sources of information and useful guides to aesthetic values. But with some exceptions they tend to be exercises in filial piety, dominated by a single-minded effort to show the subject at his best.

That is what makes Truman Bartlett's study so special. Like Rimmer, Bartlett was an art instructor; he taught at M.I.T. for nearly twenty-five years. Sensing the fragility of Rimmer's reputation, he set about not merely to record his life but to document the impact, quality, and thinking of the man as best he could. He wrote to some five hundred persons who might have known Rimmer—as teacher, colleague, physician, neighbor, artist—and reported receiving some 150 replies. These letters, some of which have already been quoted, did full justice to the strong, often acerbic, and occasionally self-destructive force of Rimmer's personality. Bartlett did not hesitate to include negative as well as positive remarks. He confronted the possibility that "conceit, self-assertion, and sensitiveness" had stunted Rimmer's development. He even speculated that Rimmer had had "no loyalty to his art instinct," but instead had used art simply as a way of earning money to support his family.[15]

But Bartlett also believed fully in Rimmer's genius, and sought to define and isolate Rimmer's aesthetic assumptions

12. *Ibid.*, p. 22. Bartlett further juxtaposed Hunt and Rimmer in the *Art Life*, pp. 79–82, and there is an illuminating summary of comparisons in Jeffrey Weidman, "William Rimmer: Critical Catalogue Raisonne" (Ph.D. Dissertation, Indiana University, 1982), 1:94–96.

13. Helen M. Knowlton, *Art Life of William Morris Hunt* (Boston: Little, Brown, 1899), p. 31. For more on Hunt see Marchal E. Landgren, *The Late Landscapes of William Morris Hunt* (College Park: University of Maryland Department of Art, 1976), and Martha J. Hoppin and Henry Adams, *William Morris Hunt: A Memorial Exhibition* (Boston: Museum of Fine Arts, 1979).

14. Little has been written about Truman Bartlett, who was the father of the sculptor Paul Wayland Bartlett. For a brief summary of his career, see Wayne Craven, *Sculpture in America* (New York: Crowell, 1968), p. 428.

15. Bartlett, *Art Life of William Rimmer*, p. 46.

and teaching objectives. Thus he included summaries of twelve of the thirty-six lectures the artist had given in Providence (newspaper summaries had already appeared), and presented a digest of Rimmer's observations as recalled by friends and students. These summaries and observations help explain something of the artist's appeal and reputation. Here are mingled specific rules about drawing and advice on technique, reflections on human and comparative anatomy, some of them radiating established conventions about racial and sexual hierarchies, confident generalizations about history and the cosmos, and eloquent appeals to idealism and the poetic spirit.[16] "All artistic races have concave faces," Rimmer announced, whereas "aggressive or conquering races have convex faces, retreating foreheads, Roman noses, and prominent chins," features belonging to both Romans and Americans. For artists, woman represented not only emotion and sentiment but also the highest representation of intellect; the "brain of woman is, proportionably, the largest of any created being." "Never use black very much," he advised students, and for beach sketching "endeavor to introduce sand-hills." "Never make a line that does not mean something. . . . Never exaggerate or overdo."

In some moments Rimmer allowed himself to be carried away by his enthusiasms. "The thigh is the noblest part of the body. . . . The knee is the finest joint in the body," he told his classes. At other times he indulged an idealist's vision of the universe. "Much of what we think belongs to the external world, belongs to ourselves. . . . While we think we are looking at the things about us . . . we are in reality looking into our own soul. . . . Trees, rocks, mountains, and valleys are beau-

tiful, only because there is in us a world of beauty, to which such things correspond." The mood and tone of his preachments, if not their actual content, echoed the fervor of his Emersonian contemporaries.

Rimmer, moreover, combined calls for personal independence, self-expression, and rebellion against rules with an insistence on discipline and careful study. Many in his audiences were not serious art students. But they could enjoy the philosophical asides, the expressions of personal opinion, and above all the masterly drawing. "Science is to art what brick-making is to architecture," Rimmer intoned; "individuality is above all." Art was not "a scholarly matter, but one of feeling and sensibility." "A work of art should be something more than the solution of a problem in science." The "faculty of reason is below the faculty of worship," he argued, urging Protestant New Englanders to heed the role of worship in Catholicism.

There was room for all, then, at Rimmer's feet. Even while he taught specific methods, he insisted that art itself was not reducible to methods. Articulate, opinionated, intense, he seemed to enjoy the challenges of educational leadership even while he chafed at the routine that teaching imposed. As a result, his influence as a pedagogue was in some ways as forceful and distinctive as his contribution to sculpture. Thanks to the devoted industry of Truman Bartlett, Rimmer's dynamism as a lecturer is caught as unmistakably as the frozen energy of his carved torsos. His words, like his best sculptures, acquire strength through their intensity and conciseness.

16. Rimmer's comments and observations are recorded by Bartlett in the *Art Life*, pp. 99–115. Many came from student notebooks acquired by Bartlett. The summaries of the Providence lectures appear on pp. 67–78.

AMERICAN MEDICINE
IN THE TIME OF WILLIAM RIMMER
Philip Cash

During the era (1840's–1860's) in which William Rimmer studied and practiced medicine the medical profession in America was beset with tension, frustration, conflict, and economic difficulty. There were five basic and interrelated causes of orthodox physicians' woes in those years: (1) a growing controversy over theory and therapy, (2) the temporarily successful challenge to regular medicine mounted by medical sects such as the botanics, the hydropaths, and the homeopaths, (3) the abandonment of the first system of state licensing of physicians, (4) the generally uneven quality of medical education, and (5) the fact that too many people were trying to earn a living practicing medicine in relation to patients' ability to pay.

During this period a majority of doctors still explained their patients' symptoms in terms of chemical and structural concepts rooted in ancient Greek thought. The chemical theory conceived of the body as containing four humors: blood, phlegm, black bile, and yellow bile. Symptoms associated with a corruption or imbalance of any of these humors could result in excessive heat, cold, wetness, or dryness, depending on which humors were affected. Advances in chemistry and physiology during the seventeenth and eighteenth centuries led to an increased emphasis on the role of blood in illness, and to a new chemical theory of disease that centered on the relative acidity of the stomach.

The structural theory postulated that the body was composed of fibers, especially the blood vessels and nerves, that it was an organism in constant flux, and that sickness was the result of excessive tensions or weakness in these fibers. Theorists differed on whether illness involved the whole body or only a particular system or organ, and on whether illnesses were specific entities or simply manifestations of a generalized pathological condition. Heredity, environment, life style, age, and sex also received heavy emphasis in all questions of sickness or health.

The therapies widely employed by most regular practitioners at this time reflected these concepts. If humoral imbalance or corruption was thought to have been produced by something in the blood, the offending "poison" should be expelled by bleeding it out, or by drugs that purged or sweated it out. If the body was excessively hot or cold, wet or dry, foods and medicines that were thought to counteract these conditions were employed. If the body's fibers were too tense or too lax, they should be relaxed by appropriate depressants or stimulated by strengthening tonics. Bleeding could also be employed to relax the circulatory system. Drugs that specifically eased pain were also in great demand. During the first half of the nineteenth century, these therapies—bleeding and purging, stimulating and depressing—were often intensified.

The confidence in these traditional theories and therapies that a majority of regular practitioners had during the period of Rimmer's medical career was based on four factors. First of all, there were the psychological forces of the weight of tradition and the natural desire of the physician to believe that his treatment made an important contribution to restoring his patient's health. Second, the true source of most illness was not known and practitioners of all schools of thought were really treating individual symptoms; many of them realized this limitation. Third, the strong therapies of most orthodox physicians did bring about physiological changes—such as vomiting or increased bowel movements—that traditional medical reasoning perceived as beneficial. Fourth, since most patients, particularly those over the age of five, recovered from their illnesses, it was understandable that physicians should attribute their patients' recoveries to the medical regimens prescribed for them.

Despite the continued widespread use of traditional therapies, the theories behind them were beginning to be undermined during the first half of the nineteenth century by new discoveries in pathology, physiology, and chemistry, by new techniques such as the use of the stethoscope and tapping the chest for telltale sounds of illness, by the development of more precise medical terminology, by the creative application of associative statistics in public health, and by attempts to relate autopsy findings to clinical symptoms. Nevertheless, modern medicine had as yet no substitute for older forms of medical thought and practice; it could only raise doubts about them. In the United States this developing therapeutic crisis was perceived mainly by the elite of the medical profession, particularly those who, like Oliver Wendell Holmes of the Harvard Medical School, had studied in Paris, then the leading center of Western medicine. Yet doubts about traditional orthodox therapies were not confined to the medical elite. More and more patients were also becoming dissatisfied with regimens that might include heavy purging, bleeding, and blistering.

This dissatisfaction with traditional medicine, along with the new spirit of democracy, reform, and free enterprise that we associate with the Age of Jackson, gave rise within a short time to a number of new medical sects. Each such sect was privately organized, dependent on charismatic leadership, and committed to some new medical dogma that resonated well with the then highly popular constellation of intuitive wisdom, practical experience, the goodness of Nature, and American nationalism. In addition, the sects had a strong appeal to many women; and because gynecology, obstetrics, and pediatrics constituted a large part of medical practice, women were in a highly strategic position to benefit a particular practitioner or medical doctrine.

The first of these sects to appear was the Thomsonians, who advocated a reliance on drugs derived from only a few plants. According to their leader, Samuel Thomson of New Hampshire, heat was the source of life and motion, and illness was almost invariably due to a loss of heat. His therapy relied on strong steam baths, hot botanicals such as cayenne pepper, and especially the potent plant evacuant *Lobelia inflata* ("Indian tobacco"), which by inducing vomiting would eliminate bodily obstructions so that properly digested food could generate heat.

Because of the simplicity of his medical doctrine and therapy, and because of his conflict with regular practitioners, Thomson asserted that a specially educated and paid medical profession was expensive, self-serving, and unnecessary. To take its place, he commissioned agents to travel throughout the nation and enroll families in his Friendly Botanic Societies for a fee of twenty dollars. Each family enrolled received a copy of Thomson's writings, to which agents would add the names of the secret ingredients of his remedies—after the fee had been paid. Although the largest numbers of Thomsonians were to be found in poor rural regions, Dr. George C. Shattuck estimated in 1828 that perhaps as many as one-sixth of the inhabitants of Boston had embraced Thomsonianism.[1]

Eventually, some of Thomson's followers broke with him and followed Alva Curtis, a former Thomsonian manager, into the Neo-Thomsonian or Physico-Medical Movement, which developed its own medical schools (generally short-lived) and professional practitioners. Most of these Neo-Thomsonians were later absorbed into another botanic sect, the Eclectics, whose most important early leader was Wooster Beach of Trumbull, Connecticut. The Eclectics were equally disenchanted with the therapeutic excesses of the regular profession

1. R. H. Fitz, "The Rise and Fall of the Licensed Physician in Massachusetts, 1781–1860," *Transactions of the Association of American Physicians,* 9 (1894): 8–9.

and the rigidity of the teachings of the other medical sects. Their motto was "Prove all things and hold to that which is good," which, however laudable as a rallying cry, offered little guidance to a physician. They relied mostly on plant medicines, from a somewhat broader spectrum than the Thomsonians used, but also occasionally prescribed mineral drugs. The Eclectics had their own medical schools and physicians. Their greatest strength was in the Middle West, where their major medical school, the Eclectic Medical Institution of Cincinnati, was located.

During the three decades before the Civil War there was a considerable affinity between medical sectarianism, feminism, and the health cult movement. Health cultists ardently advocated vegetarianism; total abstinence from alcohol, tobacco, coffee, and tea; getting plenty of fresh air, sunshine, and exercise; wearing comfortable and sensible clothing; physiological awareness, particularly among women; and mental and bodily hygiene. This movement gave us Graham flour and the Graham cracker of Sylvester Graham, a Presbyterian minister turned health crusader, and the flaking cereal and peanut butter developed by James Harvey Kellogg, who held regular and hydropathic medical degrees.

To be sure, many orthodox practitioners supported health reform, but the health cult movement as such was much more closely associated with medical sectarianism, especially the hydropaths. The founder of hydropathy was Vincenz Priessnitz, a Silesian peasant, who developed a system of treatments based on baths, douches, packs, and wet bandages. From the 1840's until the Civil War the center of hydropathy in the United States was New York City; after the war it shifted to the Seventh Day Adventist enclave at Battle Creek, Michigan. Hydropathy's most significant contribution to America was the Turkish bath. About one-fifth of hydropathic practitioners were women.[2]

The sect that offered the greatest intellectual and institutional challenge to regular medicine was homeopathy, based on the teachings of Friedrich Christian Samuel Hahnemann, a native of Meissen, Germany, who in 1779 earned an M.D. degree from the University of Erlangen. Hahnemann's medical doctrine was based on four tenets: (1) that disease is ultimately a matter of the spirit; (2) that the basic biological cause of most illness is a suppressed itch or "psora"; (3) that two diseases cannot exist in the same body at the same time and that drugs known to produce symptoms in a healthy person similar to those a sick person is suffering from will, when administered to the sick person, drive the natural disease out and restore him to health (*similia similibus curantur*); and (4) that drugs should be administered singly in tiny doses ("infinitesimals") whose potency can be greatly enhanced by shaking ("succussion" or "dynamism").

Many well-educated and thoughtful people, particularly those of a liberal bent, were attracted to homeopathy, which was introduced to America in the mid-1820's. The Massachusetts Homeopathic Fraternity, founded with four members in 1839, had over twenty by 1843, all of them regularly trained physicians and members of the Massachusetts Medical Society.[3] Although homeopaths hoped to remain a part of the regular medical profession and initially were received with sympathy by it, they were gradually driven out by orthodox practitioners (allopaths), who asserted that as adherents of a particular medical dogma they were unacceptable as members of the Society. As a result, the homeopaths developed an infrastructure of medical schools, societies, journals, dispensaries, and hospitals of their own.

Homeopathy enjoyed its greatest success in the rich urban centers of the Northeast and Middle West. Because of its emphasis on the role of the spiritual and the harmony of nature, homeopathy had a strong association with the Transcendentalist movement. Given Rimmer's ideas and his Boston and Concord associations, it seems likely that he was influenced to some extent by the homeopathic movement.

Medical sectarianism, particularly Thomsonianism, was both a primary instigator and a chief beneficiary of the abandonment of this country's first system of licensing physicians. Prior to the Revolution, only New York City (1760) and the

2. R. L. Numbers, "Do-It-Yourself the Sectarian Way," in G. B. Risse, R. L. Numbers, and J. W. Leavitt, eds., *Medicine Without Doctors: Home Health Care in American History* (New York: Science History Pubications, 1977), p. 64.
3. W. G. Rothstein, *American Physicians in the 19th Century: From Sects to Science* (Baltimore: Johns Hopkins University Press, 1972), p. 162.

colony of New Jersey (1772) had regulations licensing physicians, and New York seems never to have enforced its regulations. By the early 1830's, however, only three states lacked licensing laws. In some states, such as Massachusetts, the granting of a license to practice medicine did not exclude others from doing so, but only served to designate those deemed "duly educated and properly qualified."[4] After 1820 most states followed the example of Massachusetts and automatically licensed graduates of medical schools. The tide turned in the 1830's. By 1845, in keeping with the egalitarian and laissez-faire spirit of the times and in deference to the sectarians' criticism of orthodox medicine, ten states had repealed their licensing laws (Massachusetts did so in 1835), eight Western states had never enacted any, and only two (Louisiana and New Jersey) were attempting to regulate medical practice. By the Civil War, no state had a working licensing law.

Actually, the first state licensing system had never been very effective. County and district medical societies, the chief licensing agencies, were tempted to grant licenses liberally because of the pressure from local physicians to have their apprentices licensed and because the agencies themselves had become partially dependent on licensing fees. Also licensing laws were difficult to enforce and penalties were usually light, the chief ones being fines and denial of the right to sue to collect fees. It was under these permissive conditions that William Rimmer, with only a fragmented and highly limited formal medical training, was able to practice freely and be addressed as "Doctor Rimmer."

Another major factor in shaping American medicine in the mid-nineteenth century was the proliferation of medical schools. In 1810 there were five functioning medical schools in the United States, including those at Dartmouth and Harvard. They had 650 students, two-thirds of them at the University of Pennsylvania. By 1860 there were over forty degree-granting medical educational institutions and the number of medical students had risen to 5,000, an eightfold increase while the nation's population had grown only four and one-quarter times.[5] Not only the number but the diversity of medical schools increased dramatically: in 1860 there were orthodox, sectarian, public, private, rural, urban, and female

institutions devoted to training doctors. But the quality of medical education was diluted, and the competition for students made any improvement difficult. Also, although the increasing number of medical schools made it easier to become a doctor, the proliferation of doctors made it harder to become a prosperous one. Yet the increase continued. In Massachusetts the continued opposition of the Massachusetts Medical Society and the Harvard Medical School slowed, but did not stop, the establishment of new degree-granting medical institutions.

A substantial number of medical schools at this time were proprietary; that is, they were owned by the doctors who taught in them and were intended to make a profit (although few did). Even medical schools that were associated with colleges or universities were virtually autonomous. Almost all medical educators at this time were practicing physicians, and all courses except anatomy were taught by the lecture method. Clinical instruction was highly limited, and its true value was not widely appreciated. Most medical students of this era had not attended a liberal arts college, and those who had usually did not rank high in their class. To receive a medical degree, students were expected to attend two sets of identical lectures of 13–18 weeks' duration, although not necessarily at the same school, write a rudimentary dissertation, and pass a usually perfunctory final examination. As late as 1870 a student at Harvard Medical School had to pass only five of nine subjects in his final examination to qualify for the M.D. degree. Despite the ease of attaining a medical degree at this time, only a minority of those who attended medical school bothered to do so.

Actually, from colonial times until after the Civil War the basic form of medical education was the apprenticeship system. Medical schools had first been founded to *supplement* this training, and later they were designed to *complement* it. In

4. W. L. Burrage, *A History of the Massachusetts Medical Society, with Brief Biographies of the Founders and Chief Officers, 1781–1922* (Norwood, Mass.: privately printed, 1923).
5. J. Duffy, *The Healers: The Rise of the Medical Establishment* (New York, 1976), p. 170; W. F. Norwood, "American Medical Education from the Revolutionary War to the Civil War," *The Journal of Medical Education*, 32.6 (1967): 445; *The Statistical History of the United States from Colonial Times to the Present* (New York: McGraw-Hill and Basic Books, 1976), pp. A1–8.

1840 in New England it was still typical for medical school graduates to have spent over 80 percent of their time in medical study as the apprentice of a practicing physician.[6] The chief attractions of the apprenticeship system were its relatively low cost, the practical experience it offered, its personal nature, and the fact that it often inculcated a budding sense of professionalism. Its major defects were the lack of any controls, the narrowness of its educational focus, and the temptation for doctors to exploit their apprentices. Throughout the antebellum period a large number of physicians never received more than apprenticeship training, and for some, such as Rimmer, this training was fragmented and incomplete.

The ease with which Rimmer became a doctor highlights one important phenomenon of American medicine during his time. His failure to earn a living as a physician highlights another: the fact that far too many people were practicing medicine for the economy to sustain them. The number of physicians in the United States increased from fewer than 5,000 in 1790 to more than 40,000 in 1850; the ratio of medical practitioners to population went from $1/950$ in 1790 to less than $1/600$ in 1850.[7] Conditions were particularly bad in New England. By the early nineteenth century the region's average ratio of physicians to population was $1/522$. In Boston in 1845 it was $1/479$.[8] In 1836 the *Boston Medical and Surgical Journal* noted 16 different types of "doctors" in common practice in New England.[9] In 1854 three Harvard medical professors—hardly, to be sure, a disinterested group—estimated that Massachusetts had five times as many physicians as were needed.[10] As might be expected under these conditions, well-educated and well-connected physicians were usually able in due course to establish stable and successful practices, whereas those like Rimmer who lacked these advantages tended to emigrate, to move from place to place within the region, to combine medical practice with other work, or to leave medicine completely. Even among successful doctors, however, few were rich. During the 1830's it was estimated that few New England practitioners received more than $500 a year in money and kind.[11] In 1850 the famous Shattuck report of the Massachusetts Sanitary Commission estimated that the average Bay State physician charged fees amounting to $800 annually, but collected only $600.[12]

This was the medical world in which William Rimmer became a physician. His training was minimal even by the loose standards of the day. Between the ages of 25 and 31 (1841–47) he studied medicine intermittently and on a largely informal basis with Dr. Abel Washburn Kingman of Brockton, Massachusetts. Kingman came from a well-established South Shore family, had studied two years at Amherst College, and in 1831 had received his M.D. degree from the National Medical College of Columbian College in Washington, D.C., the forerunner of the present George Washington University School of Medicine. Why he should have traveled so far to attend a medical school of no particular distinction is puzzling. Cultured, personable, and the possessor of a good library, Kingman not only imparted his medical knowledge and insights to Rimmer, but, equally important, gave him warm encouragement and support.

Rimmer's interest in medical practice was in what he could earn by it. However, in 1843, while living temporarily in South Boston, he received an opportunity to study human anatomy directly when Dr. William T. Parker introduced him to the Harvard Medical School dissecting rooms. This was a subject of passionate interest to him, and he undoubtedly exploited his good fortune to the fullest. Beginning in the 1820's there was a growing feeling in progressive medical circles in Great Britain and America that all medical students, not just a select few, should have at least some experience in dissection rather than studying anatomy wholly by reading, lectures, and demonstrations. To effect this change it was necessary to in-

6. B. Riznik, "Medicine in New England, 1790–1840," unpublished manuscript, Old Sturbridge Village, 1965, p. 97.
7. W. Barlow and D. O. Powell, "To Find a Stand: New England Physicians on the Western and Southern Frontier, 1790–1860," *Bulletin of the History of Medicine*, 54 (1980): 386.
8. Barlow and Powell, "Stand," p. 386; Riznik, "New England," pp. 68, 75, Appendix K.
9. B. Riznik, "The Professional Lives of Early Nineteenth Century New England Doctors," *Journal of the History of Medicine and Allied Sciences*, 19 (1964): 9.
10. J. F. Kett, *The Formation of the American Medical Profession: The Role of Institutions, 1790–1860* (New Haven: Yale University Press, 1968), p. 78.
11. Riznik, "New England," p. 78.
12. P. Starr, *The Social Transformation of American Medicine: The Rise of a Sovereign Profession and the Making of a Vast Industry* (New York: Basic Books, 1982), p. 84.

crease the availability of cadavers, not an easy task given popular opposition to having bodies used for such a purpose. The Massachusetts Anatomy Act of 1831, the first of its kind in the English-speaking world, had increased the number of cadavers available by allowing unclaimed bodies that were to be buried at public expense to be turned over to qualified physicians for anatomical instruction under certain conditions. This eased the problem somewhat, but even with the liberalization of this act in 1833 and again in 1840, anatomy teachers in the Bay State still depended on professional body snatchers for many of their cadavers. In 1839 Dr. David Humphrey Storer of the Tremont Street Medical School was sorely embarrassed when the staves of a barrel containing a body he was smuggling in from New York broke loose.[13] The number of cadavers available for dissection in Massachusetts during this period seems to have fluctuated widely, and we do not know how many the Harvard dissecting rooms had at the time Rimmer was there. Still, there can be little doubt that he benefited substantially from this experience. Later he would also benefit from having access to John Collins Warren's extensive private collection of comparative anatomy materials.

It has been said that Rimmer was a member of a Suffolk Medical Society and that he received a medical diploma from it. There seems to be no evidence that such a society existed, although there may have been a small, private medical club by that name. If there was and if Rimmer did receive a diploma or certificate from it, it would have no legal and little professional significance. Only about half of the physicians in New England in his time belonged to professional societies; Dr. Kingman, for instance, was not a member of the Massachusetts Medical Society or, apparently, of any other medical society. Medical societies of Rimmer's time did perform important services. They encouraged professionalism, helped promote and disseminate medical and scientific knowledge, set standardized medical fees, and often exercised political influence. But they had no legal prerogatives and did not occupy the pivotal position in medicine that they do today.

13. Samuel Wiswell Butler to Leroy Milton Yale, Nov. 4, 1839, HMS misc., Countway Library of Medicine, Harvard Medical School.

Between about 1847 and 1863 Rimmer practiced medicine first in Randolph, then briefly in Chelsea, and finally among the quarry workers of East Milton. From what we know, he seems to have been a good doctor. Although he had an angular personality, his bedside manner was tender and reassuring. Apparently he was prudent in his use of drugs, and his cold water treatments for acute infectious diseases gained him a local reputation. Given his intelligence, manual dexterity, and keen knowledge of anatomy, he must have been an excellent surgeon.

In summary, William Rimmer as a doctor was wise and able, if economically unsuccessful and often preoccupied with other concerns. Had he become a teacher of medical anatomy, he might have been a superb one in the great Boston tradition of the Warrens and Oliver Wendell Holmes. Instead, he ultimately was able to devote his full intellect, talent, and energy to his great love: art and art anatomy. What medicine lost, art gained.

BIBLIOGRAPHY

Barlow, W., and O. W. Powell. "To Find a Stand: New England Physicians on the Western and Southern Frontier, 1790–1860," *Bulletin of the History of Medicine*, 54 (1980): 386–401.

Beecher, H. K., and M. D. Altschule. *Medicine at Harvard: The First Hundred Years.* Hanover, N.H.: University Press of New England, 1977.

Berman, A. "The Heroic Approach in 19th Century Therapeutics," *Bulletin of the American Society of Hospital Pharmacists*, 11 (1954): 320–27.

Blake, J. B. "The Development of American Anatomy Acts," *Journal of Medical Education*, 30 (1955): 431–39.

———. "Anatomy and the Congress," in L. G. Stevenson and R. P. Multhauf, eds., *Medicine, Science and Culture: Historical Essays In Honor of Owsei Temkin* (Baltimore: Johns Hopkins University Press, 1968), pp. 169–84.

———. "Health Reform," in E. S. Gausted, ed., *The Rise of Adventism: Religion and Society in Mid-Nineteenth Century America* (New York: Harper & Row, 1975), pp. 30–49.

———. "Homeopathy in American History: A Commentary," *Transactions and Studies of the College of Physicians of Philadelphia*, 5.3 (1981): 75–83.

Burrage, W. L. *A History of the Massachusetts Medical Society, with Brief Biographies of the Founders and Chief Officers, 1781–1922.* Norwood, Mass.: privately printed, 1923.

Corner, G. W. "The Role of Anatomy in Medical Education," *The Journal of Medical Education*, 33 (1968): 1–8.

Duffy, J. "The Changing Image of the American Physician," *Journal of the American Medical Association*, 200 (1967): 136–40.

———. *The Healers: The Rise of the Medical Establishment.* New York: McGraw-Hill, 1976.

Fitz, R. H. "The Rise and Fall of the Licensed Physician in Massachusetts, 1781–1860," *Transactions of the Association of American Physicians*, 9 (1894): 1–18.

Hartwell, E. M. "Anatomical Study in Massachusetts," *Annals of Anatomy and Surgery*, 3 (1881): 266–73.

Heaton, C. "Body Snatching in New York City," *New York State Journal of Medicine*, 43.19 (1943): 1861–65.

Kaufman, M. *Homeopathy in America: The Rise and Fall Of A Medical Thought.* Baltimore: Johns Hopkins University Press, 1971.

———. *American Medical Education: The Formative Years, 1765–1910.* Westport, Conn.: Greenwood Press, 1976.

Keith, N. M., and T. E. Keys. "The Anatomy Acts of 1831 and 1832, A Solution of A Medical Social Problem," A.M.A. *Archives of Internal Medicine*, 99.9 (1957): 678–94.

Kett, J. F. *The Formation of the American Medical Profession: The Role of Institutions, 1790–1860.* New Haven: Yale University Press, 1968.

Logan, S. "Hydropathy in America: A Nineteenth Century Panacea," *Bulletin of the History of Medicine*, 45 (1971): 267–80.

Norwood, W. F. *Medical Education in the United States Before the Civil War.* Philadelphia: University of Pennsylvania Press, 1944.

———. "American Medical Education from the Revolutionary War to the Civil War," *The Journal of Medical Education*, 32.6 (1967): 433–48.

Risse, G. B. Numbers, R. L., and Leavitt, J. W., eds., *Medicine Without Doctors: Home Health Care in American History.* New York: Science History Publications, 1977.

Riznik, B. "The Professional Lives of Early Nineteenth Century New England Doctors," *Journal of the History of Medicine and Allied Sciences*, 19.1 (1964): 1–16.

———. "Medicine in New England, 1790–1840." Unpublished manuscript, Old Sturbridge Village, 1965.

Rothstein, W. G. *American Physicians in the 19th Century: From Sects to Science.* Baltimore: Johns Hopkins University Press, 1972.

Shryock, R. H. *Medicine and Society in America, 1660–1860.* New York: New York University Press, 1960.

Starr, P. *The Social Transformation of American Medicine: The Rise of a Sovereign Profession and the Making of a Vast Industry.* New York: Basic Books, 1982.

Waite, F. C. "Grave Robbing in New England," *Bulletin of the Medical Library Association*, 33 (1945): 272–94.

———. "The Development of Anatomical Laws in the States of New England," *New England Journal of Medicine*, 233 (1945): 716–25.

Weiss, H. B., and H. R. Kemble, *The Great American Water-Cure Craze: A History of Hydropathy in the United States.* Trenton, N.J.: Past Time Press, 1967.

Whorton, J. C. "'Tempest in A Flesh-Pot': The Formation of a Physiological Rationale for Vegetarianism," *Journal of the History of Medicine and Allied Sciences*, 32 (1977): 115–37.

Part II CATALOG

CONVENTIONS AND ABBREVIATIONS

Jeffrey Weidman

The 85 items in the exhibition are identified in headings numbered 1–85 and are cross-referenced as "cat. 1," "cat. 2," etc. Illustrations of 20 works not included in the exhibition but reproduced in the Catalog for comparative or other purposes, including a photograph of Rimmer, are identified by legends numbered "Illustration 1," "Illustration 2," etc. and are cross-referenced as "ill. 1," "ill. 2," etc.

In dimensions, height precedes width and for sculpture the final dimension given is depth.

Illustrations are not indicated for Bibliography entries. They are listed as "ill." when found in exhibition catalogs.

The following five exhibitions are listed in the Exhibitions sections of Catalog entries in the abbreviated forms italicized below:

1880: MFA. May to mid-November 1880, Museum of Fine Arts, Boston. *Exhibition of Sculpture, Oil Paintings, and Drawings by Dr. William Rimmer.*

1883: Chase. February 1883, J. Eastman Chase Gallery, Boston. *Catalogue of Drawings, Paintings, and Sculpture by the Late Dr. William Rimmer on Exhibition and Private Sale.*

1916: MFA. Feb. 17–Mar. 1, 1916, Museum of Fine Arts, Boston. "William Rimmer Centennial Exhibition." (There was no catalog or checklist for this exhibition.)

1946/47: Whitney/MFA Nov. 5–27, 1946, Whitney Museum of American Art, NYC; Jan. 7–Feb. 2, 1947, Museum of Fine Arts, Boston. *William Rimmer, 1816–1879.* (Essay and entries by Lincoln Kirstein.)

1981: Brockton. Apr. 9–June 28, 1981, Brockton Art Museum/Fuller Memorial, Brockton, Mass. *Brockton's Artistic Heritage: An Exhibition of Historical Art by Brockton Area Artists.*

These abbreviated forms are used to refer to the catalogs as well as to the exhibitions.

Complete authors' names, titles, and publication information on works cited in short form in the Bibliography sections of Catalog entries will be found in the Bibliography, pp. 31–32. Except for Jeffrey Weidman's unpublished "William Rimmer: Critical Catalog Raisonné" (1982), which is abbreviated simply "W82," works in the Bibliography are cited by author's name and date of publication, e.g. "Bartlett 1882."

Other abbreviations used in the Catalog are as follows:

CHR   Caroline Hunt Rimmer (1851–1918), the artist's youngest daughter

ERS   Edith Rimmer Durham Simonds (Mrs. Henry Simonds, Lexington, Mass.; d. 1935), CHR's niece, heir, and executor

BML   The Boston Medical Library in the Francis A. Countway Library of Medicine

MFA   Museum of Fine Arts, Boston

NYC   New York City

BIBLIOGRAPHY

Jeffrey Weidman

Unpublished Materials

The major collections of unpublished materials concerning William Rimmer are as follows:

Boston Medical Library: Rimmer Album of poetry and drawings, holograph of "Stephen and Phillip," Stephen Higginson Perkins's letters to Rimmer, newspaper clippings scrapbook, and Hammatt Billings's sketchbook from Rimmer's spring 1864 Lowell Institute lectures

Museum of Fine Arts, Boston: registrar's and other archives

Library of Congress, Manuscript Division: papers of Paul Wayland Bartlett, Gutzon Borglum, and Daniel Chester French

Metropolitan Museum of Art, New York City: letters in the archives

Middlesex County Probate Court, Lexington, Mass.: last wills and testaments of Caroline Hunt Rimmer and of Edith Rimmer Durham Simonds

Milton Public Library, Milton, Mass.: letters between Caroline Hunt Rimmer, William R. Ware, Nathaniel T. Kidder, and others

Norfolk County Probate Court, Dedham, Mass.: last will and testament of Stephen H. Perkins

Richard S. Nutt, Providence: the Lincoln Kirstein-Richard S. Nutt research material on William Rimmer

Oberlin College Library, Special Collections: Rimmer's musical compositions

Smithsonian Institution, Archives of American Art: papers of Hiram Powers and Sadakichi Hartmann

Jeffrey Weidman, Oberlin, Ohio: letters from Lincoln Kirstein to Florence Snelling; papers of Marion M. MacLean, Rimmer's grandniece; dissertation research materials, including extensive correspondence

Whitney Museum of American Art, New York City: files on 1946 Rimmer exhibition

Published Materials and Dissertations

Armand-Dumaresque, Charles-Edouard. *Rapport sur une Mission dans l'Amérique du Nord.* Paris: Imprimerie Nationale, 1872. Reports on Rimmer's teaching at Cooper Union, 1870.

B., I. "Studios in Florence, No. I." *Once a Week,* Dec. 19, 1863, pp. 721–22.

Bartlett, Truman H. "Dr. William Rimmer," *American Art Review,* 1880; first article, pp. 461–68; second and concluding article, pp. 509–14. Reprinted in *American Art and American Art Collections* (1889), pp. 331–42, 343–52.

———. "Civic Monuments in New England, IV," *The American Architect and Building News,* July 9, 1881, pp. 15–17.

———. *The Art Life of William Rimmer: Sculptor, Painter, and Physician.* Boston: James R. Osgood and Company, 1882. The book was reprinted in 1890 by Houghton Mifflin and Company (Boston and New York) and the Riverside Press (Cambridge, Mass.) and in 1970 by Kennedy Graphics, Inc., and Da Capo Press (New York).

Borglum, Gutzon. "Our Prophet Unhonored in Art. His Sculptures Anticipated Rodin's Best—But Who Has Heard of Rimmer, Obscure Physician and Teacher of Art Anatomy," *New York Evening Post,* June 18, 1921, p. 9, cols. 1–3, and illustrations in the "Saturday Graphic" section.

Boston City Council. *Presentation of the Statue of Alexander Hamilton to the City of Boston by Thomas Lee.* Boston: Printed for the City Council, 1865.

Boston Museum. *Catalogue of the Paintings, Marble and Plaster Statuary and Engravings Comprised in The Collection of The Boston Museum and Gallery of Fine Arts.* Boston: Printed by Henry P. Lewis, 1841. Other editions by this and other printers: 1842, 1844, 1847, and 1849.

Brockton Art Museum/Fuller Memorial. *Brockton's Artistic Heritage: An Exhibition of Historical Art by Brockton Area Artists.* Brockton: Brockton Art Museum, 1981.

Champney, Benjamin. *Sixty Years' Memories of Art and Artists.* Woburn, Mass.: The News Print/Wallace and Andrews, 1900.

Chase Gallery. *Catalogue of Drawings, Paintings, and Sculpture by the Late Dr. William Rimmer on Exhibition and Private Sale.* Boston: J. Eastman Chase Gallery, 1883.

Cheney, J., and S. W. Cheney. *Outlines and Sketches by Washington Allston.* Boston: privately printed [Stephen H. Perkins], 1850.

Cooper Union. *Ninth Annual Report of the Trustees of the Cooper Union for the Advancement of Science and Art, July 1st, 1868.* New York: G. A. Whitehorne, July 1, 1868.

Craven, Wayne. *Sculpture in America*. New York: Thomas Y. Crowell Company, 1968. A New and Revised Edition was published in 1984 by the University of Delaware Press (Newark, Del.) and Cornwall Books (New York).

Cruveilhier, Jean. *The Anatomy of the Human Body*. New York: Harper & Brothers, 1847. Rimmer's annotated copy, including two drawings on pp. 474 and 521, is in the collection of the Boston Medical Library.

D., W. H. [William Howe Downes.] "The Fine Arts: Dr. Rimmer's Works Exhibition at Art Museum to Celebrate the One Hundredth Anniversary of His Birthday," *Boston Evening Transcript*, Feb. 17, 1916, n. pag. [p. 11], cols. 5–6.

Dillenberger, Jane, and Joshua C. Taylor. *The Hand and the Spirit: Religious Art in America, 1700–1900*. Berkeley: University Art Museum, 1972.

"Dr. William Rimmer," *Boston Evening Transcript*, Aug. 21, 1879, p. 8, cols. 4–5, and Aug. 22, 1879, p. 6, cols. 2–3. Obituary.

Gardner, Albert TenEyck. *Yankee Stonecutters: The First American School of Sculpture, 1800–1850*. New York: Published for the Metropolitan Museum of Art by Columbia University Press, 1945.

———. *American Sculpture: A Catalogue of the Collection of the Metropolitan Museum of Art*. New York: the Museum, 1965.

Gerdts, William H. *The Great American Nude: A History in Art*. New York: Praeger Publishers, 1974.

Goldberg, Marcia. "William Rimmer: An American Romantic Sculptor." M.A. Thesis, Oberlin College, 1972.

Hunt, William Morris. *W. M. Hunt's Talks on Art: First Series*. Boston: Houghton Mifflin and Company, and Cambridge, Mass.: The Riverside Press, 1875.

Jarves, James Jackson. *The Art-Idea*. Cambridge: The Belknap Press of Harvard University Press, 1960. Originally published in 1864.

Kirstein, Lincoln. "Who was Dr. Rimmer?," *Town & Country*, July 1946a, pp. 72–73, 118, 132–33.

——— and Whitney Museum of American Art. *William Rimmer, 1816–1879*. New York: The Museum, 1946b. Kirstein wrote the catalog entries and the essay "William Rimmer." The essay was reprinted as "William Rimmer: His Life and Art," *The Massachusetts Review*, 2.4 (Summer 1961), n. pag. [pp. 685–716].

Lovett, James D'Wolf. *Old Boston Boys and the Games They Played*. Boston: Privately printed at the Riverside Press, 1906.

Millet, F. D. "The Paintings—The Rimmer Collection," *The American Architect and Building News*, Oct. 30, 1880, pp. 212–13. Review of the MFA's 1880 Rimmer exhibition.

Museum of Fine Arts, Boston. *Exhibition of Sculpture, Oil Paintings, and Drawings by Dr. William Rimmer*. Four editions. Boston: Alfred Mudge & Son, 1880.

Opinions of Some Distinguished Artists and Connoisseurs in Reference to Dr. Rimmer's Works. Boston: publisher not known, n.d. [1864].

Perkins, Robert F., Jr., and William J. Gavin III, comps. and eds. *The Boston Athenaeum Art Exhibition Index, 1827–1874*. Boston: The Library of the Boston Athenaeum, 1980.

Pierce, H. Winthrop. *The History of the School of the Museum of Fine Arts, Boston, 1877–1927*. Boston: Museum of Fine Arts, 1930.

Providence Daily Journal. Twenty-six articles (reports) of Rimmer's three series of lectures in Providence in 1871–73. Weidman, "William Rimmer" (see below), 1:125–26, lists each article.

R. [William Rimmer]. "The Love Chant: A Satire," *Sunday Herald*, Boston, Jan. 8, 1874.

Rimmer, William. *Elements of Design*. Boston: Printed by John Wilson and Son, 1864. A second, revised edition, with an added part VI, on "Form," was published in 1879 as *Elements of Design in Six Parts* (Boston: Lee & Shepard Publishers, and New York: Charles T. Dillingham). This was reprinted in 1891 and 1907. Part VI reflects, in part, material in Rimmer's 1877 *Art Anatomy*.

———. "To the Editor of the Sun," *New York Sun*, June 3, 1868.

———. *Art Anatomy*. Boston: Little, Brown and Company, 1877. Later American editions were published by Houghton Mifflin and Company (Boston and New York) and the Riverside Press (Cambridge, Mass.) in 1884, 1889, 1893, and 1905. An edited and rearranged edition was published in 1962 by Dover Publications (New York). There was also a London edition, published by Kegan Paul, Trench & Co. in 1884.

Sarmiento, Domingo Faustino. *Cartas de Sarmiento à la señora Maria Mann*. Buenos Aires: Academia Argentina de Letras, 1936.

Stebbins, Theodore E., Jr. *American Master Drawings and Watercolors: A History of Works on Paper from Colonial Times to the Present*. New York: Harper & Row in association with The Drawing Society, Inc., 1976.

———, Carol Troyen, and Trevor J. Fairbrother. *A New World: Masterpieces of American Painting, 1760–1910*. Boston: Museum of Fine Arts, 1983.

Swan, Mabel Munson. *The Athenaeum Gallery, 1827–1873*. Boston: The Boston Athenaeum, 1940.

Troyen, Carol. *The Boston Tradition: American Paintings from the Museum of Fine Arts, Boston*. New York: American Federation of Arts, 1980.

Tuckerman, Henry Theodore. *Book of the Artists*. New York: G. P. Putnam & Son, 1867.

Walters, Charles Thomas. "Hiram Powers and William Rimmer: A Study in the Concept of Expression." Ph.D. dissertation, University of Michigan, 1977. Published by Ann Arbor: University Microfilms International, 1977.

Weidman, Jeffrey. "William Rimmer: Critical Catalogue Raisonné." Ph.D. dissertation, Indiana University, 1982. 7 vols.; 1,905 pages. Published by Ann Arbor: University Microfilms International, 1982.

———. "William Rimmer: Creative Imagination and Daemonic Power," in *The Art Institute of Chicago Centennial Lectures: Museum Studies 10* (Chicago: Contemporary Books, 1983), pp. 146–63.

Winsor, Justin, ed. *The Memorial History of Boston, 1630–1880*. Boston: James R. Osgood and Company, 1881.

Zeros [William Rimmer]. "Autumn," *Boston Journal*, Sept. 20, 1858.

SCULPTURE

1. Horse Pulling Stone-Laden Cart

c. 1828–c. 1832

Marble with touches of paint on hooves and harness,
6 × 17 × 10 in. (15.25 × 43.20 × 25.40 cm).
Signed, at back, below horse's right front leg:
W. Rimmer.

S. Grant Waters. Bought at Maryland antique show
between 1967 and 1970.

Provenance. Anonymous private dealer, Boston.

Bibliography. May 1973; Adam A. Weschler & Son,
Washington, D.C., sales catalog, p. 91, 1023b.
June 17, 1984; *Auction of Important Fine Art and
Antiques: The Collection of S. Grant Waters, Balti-
more, Maryland,* William H. Amos–Glen Freeman,
Auctioneers, 244 (ill.). W82, pp. 140–41.

This earliest known sculpture by William Rimmer was intended as an inkwell. The use of the
base as an integral part of the composition and
its textural contrast with the main figure are
found in another early sculpture, *Seated Man*
(cat. 2). The subject, material, and style are recognizable in Rimmer's other early work. The
small size, anatomical accuracy, expressive
quality, and combination of imaginative and
utilitarian form are consistent with the young
Rimmer's avenues of artistic expression. The
element of pathos is a hallmark of his finest
sculptures.

2. Seated Man

1831–1832

Gypsum, 10¼ × 7¾ × 4¼ in. (26.05 × 19.70 × 10.80 cm)

Museum of Fine Arts, Boston, 20.210. Gift of ERS, Mar. 4, 1920.

Provenance. CHR, then ERS.

Exhibitions. Perhaps 1838: Colton's Art Store on Tremont St., Boston. 1883: Chase, 93. 1916: MFA. 1946/47: Whitney/MFA, 1 (ill.).

Bibliography. Bartlett 1880, pp. 464, 465. Bartlett 1882, pp. 5–6, 15, 49. Feb. 10, 1917: will of CHR, Article X, leaves figure to the "National Gallery at Washington," the "Smithsonian Institute"—refused in 1919. Borglum 1921. Gardner 1945, pp. 38, 70. Kirstein 1946b, p. 3. Craven 1968, pp. 347–48, 355. W82, pp. 141–50.

Seated Man, whose face resembles Thomas Rimmer's, reveals the adolescent William Rimmer's insight into his father's isolation and emotional turmoil. Despite the stabilizing effect of the base, the naked figure remains exposed and vulnerable. The choice of gypsum, which appears strong and durable but is in fact quite fragile, may have been symbolic, like the choice of granite for Rimmer's later sculpture *St. Stephen* (ill. 2, p. 38).

Seated Man may be the first stone nude figure carved in America. It exhibits Rimmer's dexterity in rendering anatomy in a plastic medium and his precocious use of composition to convey a highly charged emotional state. His ability to suggest the tension of muscles beneath the skin places Rimmer in a class apart from his American contemporaries.

The haunting image of *Seated Man* (called *Despair* by Truman Bartlett) recalls Michelangelo's *Last Judgement*, which Rimmer might have known through prints. If so, he has transformed it into a powerful three-dimensional form that presages his finest work.

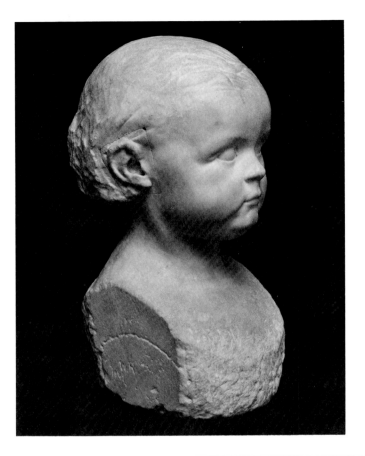

3. Mary Rimmer

1849

Marble, 13½ × 7 × 7½ in. (34.28 × 17.85 × 19.08 cm). Signed and dated, on flat side of right shoulder: W. R. / 1849.

Boston Medical Library. Gift of ERS, 1920, on or after Feb. 5.

Provenance. CHR, then ERS.

Exhibition. 1883: Chase, 92. 1916: MFA. 1946/47: Whitney/MFA, 2. 1981: Brockton, 3.

Bibliography. May 3, 1861: letter from Stephen H. Perkins to Hiram Powers. Bartlett, 1880, p. 465. Bartlett, 1882, p. 20. Feb. 10, 1917: will of CHR, Article X, leaves this work to "National Gallery at Washington," the "Smithsonian Institute"—refused in 1919. Kirstein, 1946b, p. 6. Craven 1968, pp. 348–49. W82, 150–53.

This is the first sculpture Rimmer made after *Seated Man* (cat. 2), some eighteen years earlier. The work was not commissioned; Rimmer may have worried that his three-year-old daughter would succumb to the fate of three of her brothers, who had all died in infancy, and sought on that account to capture her face. He exploited the translucent quality of marble to convey the soft flesh of a young face.

The pupilless eyes, consistent with Neoclassical conventions of the Ideal, heighten the sense of transiency. The frontal gaze and somber expression are alleviated by a slight turn of the head to the left and the unsymmetrical treatment of the hair. Either owing to a shortness in the original block (as suggested by Bartlett) or to correct an error, a square area containing the right ear was set into the marble.

As with other sculptures, Rimmer's method was direct; no preliminary studies in any medium survive. His working method was informal: sitting on the floor, he observed his daughter as she played beside him.

4. Head of a Woman

c. 1859

Granite, 25 × 9¹⁄₁₆ × 9⅜ in (63.50 × 23.00 × 23.80 cm). Height includes pedestal base of 6 in. (15.75 cm).

Corcoran Gallery of Art, Washington, D.C., 20.4. Gift of ERS, Oct. 29, 1920 (as executor of CHR's will).

Provenance. CHR.

Exhibitions. 1883: Chase, 95. 1916: MFA. Nov. 13–Dec. 20, 1949: Watkins Gallery of American University, Washington, D.C., *19th and 20th Century Sculpture.* Sept. 11–Nov. 15, 1970: Sheldon Memorial Art Gallery, University of Nebraska, Lincoln, *American Sculpture,* 132.

Bibliography. May 3, 1861: letter from Stephen H. Perkins to Hiram Powers. Bartlett, 1880, p. 465. Bartlett, 1882, p. 27. Feb. 10, 1917: will of CHR, Article X, leaves this work to "National Art Gallery at Washington, D.C.," the "Smithsonian Institute"—refused in 1919. 1949: Charles Seymour, Jr. *Tradition and Experiment in Modern Sculpture,* pp. 40, 43. Mar. 1956: University Prints, H 305. Craven 1968, p. 353. W82, pp. 157–63.

Although this sculpture bears some resemblance to Rimmer's wife, Mary, it was not intended as a representation of her. It was cut directly from the block without any preliminary studies. *Head of a Woman,* Rimmer's first surviving sculpture since the 1849 bust of his daughter Mary (cat. 3), was done at a time when he hoped sculpture would supplement his meager income from practicing medicine.

Rimmer has classicized his material, notably the high bridge of the nose. The blank eyes stem from contemporary Neoclassical convention, and the pedestal base may have been inspired by antique sculpture.

Despite its idealizing qualities, *Head of a Woman* remains a representation of a contemporary woman, with its strong, full features somewhat softened by a cluster of flowers at the side of the head. The complex interplay of hair and flowers contrasts with the more simplified treatment of the face. The blank eyes lend an air of self-absorption slightly tinged with a wistful melancholic expression. The sculpture is enlivened by flecks of mineral in the stone, especially in the cleft of the upper lip, and by the head's downward tilt and turn to the left.

The entry in the 1883 Chase Gallery catalog dismissed this sculpture as merely a technical prelude to the 1860 *St. Stephen* (ill. 2, p. 38), but it is a mature and successful sculpture in its own right, with exquisitely delicate modeling. Indeed, it can be viewed as the feminine counterpart of the masculine *St. Stephen* in its sureness of conception, design, and execution.

St. Stephen (ill. 2)
1860

Granite, 21¾ × 13⅛ × 15 in. (55.30 × 33.30 × 38.10 cm). Signed and dated, below right shoulder: W. Rimmer/1860. Inscribed, in a rectangular area at the front of the base: Stephen.

The Art Institute of Chicago, Roger McCormick Fund, 1977.23. Purchased in August 1977 from Richard S. Nutt. Unavailable for exhibition owing to fragile condition.

Provenance. Stephen Higginson Perkins bought this sculpture from the artist for $150 sometime before having it sent to Europe in 1862. He bequeathed it to the MFA, which acquired it in 1878. The MFA deaccessioned it in 1936, whereupon, as directed in Perkins's will, it went to Mrs. Charles M. Cabot. Mrs. Cabot's heirs gave it to a charity institution, the Morgan Memorial, Boston, which sold it to Mr. and Mrs. William J. Gunn, Newtonville, Mass. In May 1958 it was purchased from the estate of Marion Raymond Gunn by Richard S. Nutt, Providence, R.I.

Exhibitions. Dec. 1860: Williams and Everett's Art Gallery, Boston. Oct.–early Nov. (?) 1862: unidentified London exhibition. May 1863: Salon des Refusés, Paris. Early October 1863 possibly to fall of 1877: Perkins's studio, Florence. 1880: MFA, 4. 1916: MFA. 1946/47: Whitney/MFA, 3 (ill.). Mar. 1–29, 1968: Boston University School of Fine and Applied Arts, *Boston Painters 1720–1940,* 68. Apr. 25–June 16, 1968: Yale University Art Gallery, *American Art from Alumni Collections,* 90.

Bibliography. Dec. 12, 1860: C., "Dr. Rimmer's Head of St. Stephen: To the Editor of the Boston Journal," *Boston Daily Journal,* p. 4. Dec. 14, 1860: letter from Stephen H. Perkins to Rimmer. May 3, 1861: letter from Stephen H. Perkins to Hiram Powers. Nov. 15, 1862, July 11 and Oct. 14, 1863: letters from Stephen H. Perkins in Florence to Rimmer. I. B. 1863, pp. 721–22. *Opinions* 1864: pp. 2, 3, 4, 6, 8. Jarves 1864: p. 221. Jan. 10 and June 26, 1864: letters from Perkins to Rimmer. Tuckerman 1867: pp. 593–94. June 21, 1875: third codicil to will of Stephen H. Perkins (Aug. 2, 1861), Florence, pp. 17–18, calls for MFA to select works of art, among which is named "7 Granite head by Dr. Rimmer." Bartlett 1880, pp. 461, 465, 467, [509]. Bartlett 1882, pp. v, 26, 29–31, 33, 36, 37, 49, 136, 145. 1903: Lorado Taft, *The History of American Sculpture,* p. 187. Borglum 1921. Gardner 1945, pp. 38, 70. Kirstein 1946*b*, pp. 7–8, 9. Craven, 1968: pp. 349–50, 351, 355. Weidman 1983, pp. 147–53, 160–61. W82, pp. 163–87.

St. Stephen, a pivotal work in Rimmer's career, marked his debut as a serious artist. Significantly, it altered his self-image from that of a country doctor who occasionally produced a work of art to that of a man whose primary calling was artistic creation.

The busts by Rimmer that precede and follow *St. Stephen,* such as *Mary Rimmer* and *Head of a Woman* (cat. 3 and 4) and *Horace Mann* and *Abraham Lincoln* (ill. 3 and 4) cannot compare in power and intensity with this work. In conceiving *St. Stephen,* Rimmer probably had several sources in mind, including Washington Allston's 1812 painting *The Angel Releasing St. Peter from Prison,* a cast of the bust of *Homer,* and, most importantly, a cast of the *Laocoön,* all of which he could have seen at the Boston Athenaeum on October 8, 1860, shortly before beginning work on the piece. Although Rimmer derived some of the Saint's features from the *Laocoön,* the emotional content suggests not desperation but a transcendance of corporeal death. The suffering gaze suggests both tragedy and forgiveness, as in the martyr's final words, "Lord, lay not this sin to their charge." (*Acts of the Apostles* 7:60.)

Although the subject was selected partially in deference to the saintly namesake of Stephen Perkins, the emotional force of the image derives from Rimmer's identification with St. Stephen's sufferings. He had depicted St. Stephen's martyrdom in two works from around 1845, a lost painting and a drawing (ill. 5). A character by the same name was also a principal figure in Rimmer's prose narrative "Stephen and Phillip," which deals with man's daemonic nature imprisoned in the body. On p. 171 of "Stephen and Phillip," Stephen states: "Alas . . . a man's grief is often his only fortune, and his sorrow like his poverty the only indication of his life. This is all that is left one, and to forget it would be to lose all that I have, the sense that preserves to me my only companion, myself."

Considering his poverty at this time, it is remarkable that Rimmer decided to work on a sculpture for which there was no commission. The selection of granite for an indoor sculpture was

ILL. 2. *St. Stephen. Courtesy of The Art Institute of Chicago.*

ILL. 3. *Bust of Horace Mann*, 1866–1867. Marble; height including pedestal 26 in. (66 cm). *Courtesy of the Museo Historico Sarmiento, Buenos Aires.*

ILL. 4. *Bust of Abraham Lincoln*, 1866–1867. Marble; height including pedestal 26¾ in. (68 cm). *Courtesy of the Museo Historico Sarmiento, Buenos Aires.*

unconventional. Rimmer's choice was no doubt primarily based on what was readily available from the local quarries, but the exceptionally obdurate nature of the material carried symbolic meaning for him as well. The act of carving it—without models or preparatory sketches, working directly on a barrelhead in his woodhouse with tools that needed constant sharpening, during a four-week period beginning in early November in which many other responsibilities claimed his time—was highly exacting and provided a kind of catharsis. The handicaps under which he worked, however, are not apparent in the finished bust. *St. Stephen* is a highly controlled work with bold form, subtle modeling, and linear accents. Dynamic animation from composition, chisel marks, and exploitation of the mineral content give the bust a sense of spontaneity.

The composition encourages the viewer to move around the work. This conception of sculpture as three-dimensional form to be experienced in the round was already apparent in Rimmer's *Seated Man* (cat. 2) of thirty years before. The subtle surface modulations, the emotional expression, and the suggestion of movement engage our attention and demand both intellectual and emotional involvement. *St. Stephen*, like the later *Dying Centaur* (cat. 6), is not meant for passive contemplation but for provocative confrontation. A symbolic self-portrait, it is a shattering expression of anguish personified.

ILL. 5. *The Stoning of St. Stephen*, c. 1845. Pencil, India ink, and ink wash on beige paper; 12 × 17 in. (30.05 × 44.45 cm). *Courtesy of Mrs. R. Rex Price.*

5. Falling Gladiator
1861

Plaster (original); bronze (1907 cast), 63¼ × 42⅞ × 42⅝ in. (160.68 × 108.90 × 108.25 cm). Signed and inscribed, on top of base, between the feet: W. Rimmer/Sc. The original plaster cast was begun on Feb. 4, 1861, and completed on June 10. Two bronze casts were made sometime after June 11, 1907, this being the second sculpture by Rimmer cast in bronze under the auspices of the Rimmer Memorial Committee (see Chronology, 1905). The Metropolitan Museum of Art owns the first; the second, cataloged here, is owned by the MFA. The original plaster cast is owned by the National Museum of American Art, Washington, D.C.; gift of CHR, 1915. The caster's mark, in oval impression on the front edge of the base below the first "m" in the signature, is now illegible on the MFA bronze. The mark on the Metropolitan Museum of Art's cast:: P. P. Caproni & Bro. Plaster Casts, Boston. The founder's mark, on top of the base, one inch behind the center of the right edge of the right foot: JNO. WILLIAMS. INC./BRONZE FOUNDRY N.Y.

Museum of Fine Arts, Boston, 08.74. Gift of CHR, Mrs. Adeline Rimmer Durham, Mrs. James K. Barnard, Miss E. H. Bartol, Miss Mary D. Bates, Mrs. E. M. Cory, Mrs. C. P. Coffin, Mrs. C. A. Cummings, Mrs. Edward Cunningham, Miss Hester, Miss S. B. Fay, Mrs. A. W. Elson, Mrs. W. H. Hughes, Mr. N. T. Kidder, Miss Minns, Mrs. Daniel Merriman, Miss C. L. Parsons, Miss E. W. Perkins, and Mrs. A. C. Wheelwright, Jan. 9, 1908.

Provenance. Rimmer Memorial Committee, then CHR *et al.*

Exhibitions. PLASTER CASTS. After June 10, 1861: Rimmer's home in East Milton. Nov. 1861–summer 1866: Studio Building and various other Boston locations. May–June, 1863: Salon des Refusés, Paris (Perkins's cast). May–June, 1866: National Academy of Design, NYC, "1866 Annual Exhibition," 542. 1866–fall 1872: Cooper Union, NYC. 1880: MFA, 1. Mar. 1909–late Apr. 1915: Milton Public Library, Milton, Mass. BRONZE. 1916: MFA. 1946/47: Whitney/MFA, 4.

Bibliography (all entries but one are for the original plaster cast and the cast Perkins had in Europe). May 3 and Nov. 2, 1863: letters from Stephen H. Perkins to Hiram Powers in Florence. Oct. 3 and Nov. 15, 1862, and June 3 and 18, July 11, Sept. 9, and Oct. 14, 1863: letters from Perkins in Florence to Rimmer. I.B. 1863, pp. 721–22. *Opinions 1864*. Jarves 1864, p. 221. Tuckerman 1867, p. 59. July 6, 1867: "Die Cooper-Union Zeichene-Schule fur Frauenzimmer," *Frank Leslie's Illustrirte Zeitung*; repro. p. 360 of Rimmer's Cooper Union studio shows the *Gladiator*.

Feb. 29, 1868: "Dr. Rimmer's Statues at the Cooper Institute Art School," *Watson's Art Journal*, p. 254. Bartlett 1880, pp. 462, 465–67, [509]. Bartlett 1882, pp. v, 31–34, 37, 38, 48, 49, 121, 124, 136, 145. Jan. 26, 1906–Apr. 23, 1915: 22 letters between CHR and officials of the Milton Public Library regarding its exhibition there. Kirstein 1946*b*, pp. 1, 8–9, 10, 15, 17 (plaster) and pp. 1, 14, 16 (bronze). Gardner 1965, p. 14. Craven 1968, pp. 350, 351, 355. Nov. 1979: Marcia Goldberg, "An American in Paris: William Rimmer's *Falling Gladiator* in the Salon des Refusés," *Gazette des Beaux Arts*, pp. 175–82. W82, pp. 187–232.

In January 1861 Rimmer received $100 from Stephen Perkins to begin work on the life-sized statue of the *Falling Gladiator*. Owing to the attention *St. Stephen* had received, Rimmer had become somewhat of a curiosity; and as a consequence his work on the *Gladiator* was intermittently interrupted by friends and acquaintances of Perkins. These interruptions compounded Rimmer's difficulties in his cramped, poorly lit, and inadequately heated basement studio, where his clay froze and fell, after which it had to be shored up with stakes. Finally, the work was cast in plaster and the statue finished in that material. Despite these primitive working conditions and methods, the interruptions, and the continuing responsibilities of his medical practice, Rimmer managed to salvage some 200 hours of working time for the statue and completed it in about four months. Using no preparatory sketches or models, he worked with prodigious concentration, determination, and speed.

The result was a masterly transformation of Classical, Renaissance, and modern sources into a formal and symbolic whole that powerfully expresses Rimmer's sculptural genius. Combining naturalistic anatomical detail with an idealized head and abstract genitals, the statue is suffused with a suggestion of motion and an intensity of feeling very unlike any other American sculpture of the period.

In the *Gladiator* Rimmer reconciled contrasting themes and forms. The right side of the body, sweeping and straining upward, is countered by the compressed and falling left side, a movement slightly reduced by the necessary support. Despite the seemingly falling posture of the figure, the intricate balance of arms and legs is maintained from all sides to create a rich interplay of contrasting and complementary forms.

The simultaneous contrasting movements of the body in two opposite directions enhance the statue's intensity of feeling and dramatic impact. The body does not collapse but, like the *Dying Centaur* (cat. 6) and the various versions of *Evening, or the Fall of Day* (cat. 63 and 84; ill. 18), hovers at the intersection of two compositional spirals. The arrangement of echoed forms compels the viewer to circle the statue and encounter new combinations of solids and voids.

The muscles of the statue are taut but not exaggerated. Rimmer's immense anatomical knowledge and superb sculptural sense led him to avoid rendering the body as if it had been flayed; it is not an *écorché*. The surface has an expressive vitality, seen well in both the plaster and bronze versions. From its contracted toes to its clenched fists, the statue's details, surface treatment, and composition are used to express the passage from life to death.

Although Rimmer's anatomical knowledge had made it possible for him to forgo executing a preliminary model for the *Gladiator*, the work is not without antecedents. He undoubtedly was influenced by plaster casts of certain Hellenistic representations of the male nude that expressed an ideal of heroic beauty, such as the *Dying Gaul* (known then as the *Dying Gladiator*), the *Borghese Warrior* (known then as the *Gladiator Borghese*), and the *Torso Belvedere*. Rimmer's *Gladiator*, however, is neither an imitation nor a pastiche of these works.

Unlike the work of Rimmer's American contemporaries, the *Falling Gladiator* is essentially nonprogrammatic, nondidactic, and nonliterary. The *Gladiator's* three-dimensional plastic power, its tactile surface treatment, and its expressionistic realization were revolutionary and foreshadow the work of Auguste Rodin.

If *St. Stephen* was a kind of self-portrait, the *Gladiator* may be seen as a symbolic portrait of the artist's father. In his manuscript "Stephen and Phillip" Rimmer alluded to his father through the metaphor of the gladiator: "And I looked at him with many bitter thoughts as one might look upon the son of a great King who knowing not his heritance, was a Gladiator having no calling but to shed his blood at other's will; looked at him with compassion." A number of writers have seen the *Gladiator* as symbolic of Thomas Rimmer's death; more accurately it can be seen as a symbolic representation of his father's tragic life.

The personal symbolism of the statue is not obvious or even important to the casual viewer. A broader interpretation might place the figure as a kind of Christian soldier related to the outbreak of the Civil War on April 13, 1861. Parallels can also be found in David Scott's mid-nineteenth-century illustrations to John Bunyan's *The Pilgrim's Progress*.

The *Falling Gladiator*, the summation of Rimmer's youth and maturity, is a complex amalgamation of form and symbol. The personal and the universal, the secrets of a private history and the intimations of a national one, have become one. The tremendous concentration of energies in this sculpture seems to have sapped Rimmer's strength. His work of the next two decades did not decline in quality, but he never again attempted or achieved anything as all-consuming or on as monumental a scale.

6. Dying Centaur
1869

Plaster (original); bronze (1905/6 cast), 21½ × 25 × 23½ in. (54.60 × 66.30 × 59.70 cm). Signed, on top of base, between the hooves: W. Rimmer. The original plaster cast was made c. January–April, 1869. The bronze cast was made between the fall of 1905 and mid-January 1906; this was the first sculpture by Rimmer cast under the auspices of the Rimmer Memorial Committee (see Chronology, 1905). Founder's mark, behind right hind leg: GORHAM·CO·FOUNDERS.

Metropolitan Museum of Art, 06.146. Gift of Edward Holbrook, after Mar. 20 and before Apr. 11, 1906. The original plaster cast is at the MFA (19.127); bequest of CHR.

Provenance. Gorham Company (Foundry), then Edward Holbrook, President, Gorham Company.

Exhibitions. May 27, 1869: Cooper Union School of Design for Women, NYC, "Annual Exhibition." Mar. or Apr. 1871: Boston Art Club. 1880: MFA, 2. 1883: Chase, 94. 1946/47: Whitney/MFA, 5 (bronze). Apr. 9–Oct. 17, 1965: Metropolitan Museum of Art, *Three Centuries of American Painting*, K-7 (bronze). Sept. 28–Nov. 27, 1966: Whitney Museum of American Art, *Art of the United States: 1670–1966*, 347 (bronze), ill. Nov.–Dec. 1973: MFA, *Confident America: Monuments in Painting, Sculpture, Prints and Other Arts* (plaster). Mar. 14–Apr. 13, 1975: University of Texas at Arlington, *Figure and Field in America* (bronze), ill. Mar. 16–Sept. 26, 1976: Whitney Museum of American Art, *200 Years of American Sculpture*, 205 (bronze), ill.

Bibliography. June 2, 1869: W., "Dr. Rimmer," *Boston Daily Evening Transcript*, p. 2, col. 3. Bartlett 1882, pp. 124, 136. Dec. 13 and 15, 1905, and Jan. 19, 1906: letters between Daniel Chester French and Gutzon Borglum. Feb. 10, 1917: will of CHR, Article IX, leaves original plaster to MFA. Borglum 1921 (plaster). Kirstein 1946b, pp. 1, 15 (plaster). Gardner 1965, pp. 14, 15. Craven 1968, pp. 355, 356. Gerdts 1974, pp. 101, 102. Mar.–Apr. 1977: Milo M. Naeve, "A Picture and Sculpture by William Rimmer," *Bulletin of the Art Institute of Chicago*, pp. 18–20; on Art Institute's 1967 copyrighted Kennedy Galleries bronze cast. Weidman 1983, pp. 147, 154–63. W82, pp. 307–56.

Rimmer's plaster of the *Dying Centaur*, from the spring of 1869, marks his return to expressive, dynamic sculpture, which he had not fully explored since his *Falling Gladiator* (cat. 5) of 1861. In the intervening years he had conceived or attempted a number of works that were at least superficially reposeful, of which only the

Alexander Hamilton (frontispiece) survives. At the end of the decade he returned to the mode more suited to his talents. Choosing a classical theme, but an unusual one for a sculptor in America, Rimmer made the *Dying Centaur* an expressive vehicle for symbolic content.

Although Rimmer's *Centaur* may be the first sculpture of this subject done in America, it was a popular theme in Europe. Possible sources for the work include an illustration of a Lapith and Centaur metope from the Parthenon published in Stuart and Revett's *The Antiquities of Athens* (1762–94), Antoine-Louis Barye's mid-1840's versions of *Theseus Slaying the Centaur Bianor*, Antonio Canova's 1819 *Theseus Slaying the Centaur*, and Samuel F. B. Morse's painting (1812–13) and sculpture (1812) of *Dying Hercules*. The *Centaur* invokes all these works and with characteristic boldness demands comparison with them.

Like Rimmer's other fine sculptures, such as *Seated Man* (cat. 2), *St. Stephen* (ill. 2), *Falling Gladiator* (cat. 5), and *Fighting Lions* (cat. 7), the *Dying Centaur* is a work of contrasts reconciled. The composition is based on opposing lines of movement, which function as a spiral and lock the figure into a hovering balance. The contrast of the heavy body, which seems to press into the physical world, with the upraised face and arm, which seem to aspire to a celestial one, creates tension and power.

Part of the *Centaur's* strength, as with Rimmer's other sculptures, derives from the richness of experiencing it from many vantage points. When the sculpture is viewed in the round, the seemingly impotent quality of the arms is mitigated by the dynamic composition and the suggestive power of the torso.

The *Dying Centaur* is far from a mere exercise in anatomical ingenuity. Rimmer was dedicated to anatomical fidelity not for its own sake but for the dramatic power it enabled him to achieve. The stress of the accurately rendered anatomical parts is harmonized with an expression of the figure's inherent agony. This dramatic power is enhanced by the rippling surface animated by highlights and shadows. Although more apparent in bronze, the effect is still visible in plaster.

Rimmer's choice of subject indicates commitment to a Greek ideal. On the whole, the centaur symbolized man's sensual nature for the ancients, and was often depicted as a bestial creature. Rimmer invokes the Greek ideal by the youthful body, calm face, and the truncated limbs, which imitate antique sculptural fragments and convey a sense of tragedy. The difference between Rimmer's conception and the Greek one is that the human and animal parts of Rimmer's centaur are not at odds but in harmony with one another.

A number of specific symbolic interpretations of the *Dying Centaur* have been suggested for this reconciliation of man's animal and human natures. For example, Rimmer may have been referring to the sacrifice of the men who perished in the Civil War. In this light the *Centaur* would allude to Chiron, teacher of Achilles, who volunteered to die in the place of Prometheus. Rimmer's characterization of the Centaur as a youthful, beardless figure ties the sculpture to the young men who gave their lives in the war. As their deaths contributed to the salvation of the nation, so the death of this centaur will lead to the salvation of its soul.

Rimmer's work on the *Dying Centaur* may also have reflected the difficulties he experienced during the spring of 1869 at Cooper Union. Schooled in medicine and the arts, Chiron could have been seen by Rimmer as a mythological analogue to himself as a teacher-artist-physician who, faced with an uncomprehending public, sacrificed his own material comforts for the sake of art.

Yet it would be shortsighted and inconsistent with Rimmer's other work to view the *Centaur* as a mere embodiment of his personal frustrations and disappointments. Whatever it may say on this score, it is also an objective statement of his artistic purpose and his views on the nature of man. An optimistic work, it confirms Rimmer's belief in man's harmonious totality. As with the earlier *St. Stephen* (ill. 2), the *Dying Centaur* is a summation of many currents transfused into one powerful statement.

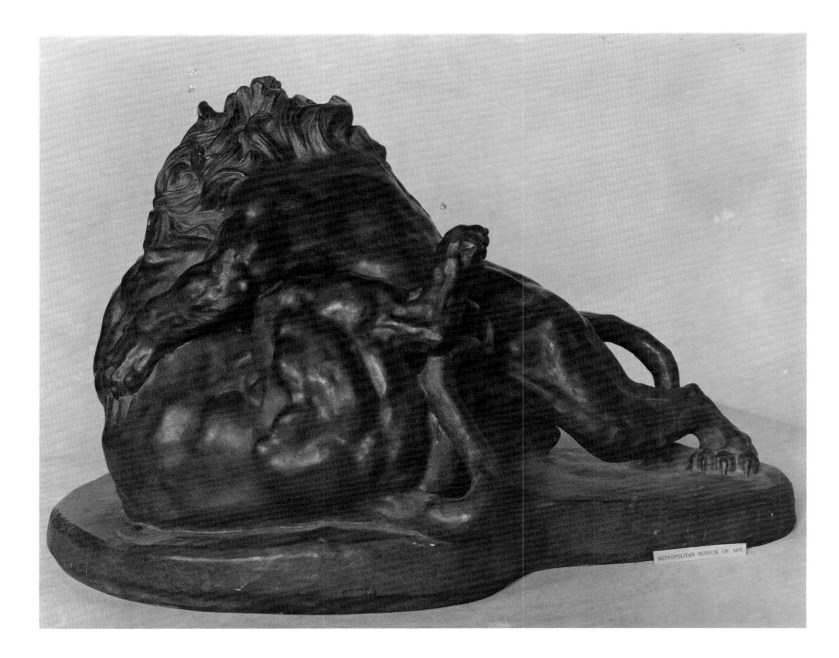

METROPOLITAN MUSEUM OF ART.

44

7. Fighting Lions

1870–1871

Plaster, bronzed (also called "verd antique") sometime after Rimmer's death; bronze (1907 cast), 16½ × 26 × 20 in. (41.93 × 66.30 × 50.80 cm). Signed, on top of base, behind the lions, below area of male lion's left knee: W. Rimmer. The original plaster cast was made c. November 1870–c. spring 1871. The bronze cast was made before Oct. 20, 1907; this was the third sculpture by Rimmer cast under the auspices of the Rimmer Memorial Committee (see Chronology, 1905). Founder's mark, on vertical surface of base, below male lion's tail and left paw: JNO. WILLIAMS, INC./BRONZE FOUNDRY/N.Y.

Metropolitan Museum of Art, 07.223. Gift of Daniel Chester French, between Sept. 20 and Oct. 20, 1907. (The whereabouts of the original plaster is unknown; it was owned by the Boston Art Club in 1947.)

Provenance. Rimmer Memorial Committee, then Daniel Chester French.

Related works. Pencil drawing of *Fighting Lions*, 1866–69, eighth sheet in the Bates Sketchbook (BML). Lost *Leaf (Sheet) of Sketches*, c. November 1870, with three groups of fighting lions (see W82, pp. 992–94).

Exhibitions. c. 1871: Williams and Everett's Art Gallery, Boston, lent by the artist. Jan. 12–Feb. 5, 1876: Boston Art Club, *First Exhibition of 1876*, 205, lent by the Club. 1880: MFA, 3. 1916: MFA. 1946/47: Whitney/MFA, 6 (bronze), ill.; while the exhibition was at the MFA, the original plaster was shown at the Boston Art Club. Sept. 28–Nov. 27, 1966: Whitney Museum of American Art, *Art of the United States: 1670–1966*, 348 (bronze). June 29–Aug. 25, 1974: Queens Museum, *The Artist's Menagerie: Five Millennia of Animals in Art*, 116 (bronze). Nov. 1975–Nov. 1976: Elvehjem Art Centre, U. of Wisconsin, Madison, *American Sculpture from the Metropolitan Museum of Art, New York.*

Bibliography. Bartlett 1880, p. 468. Bartlett 1882, pp. 95, 124, 136. Gardner 1945, p. 70 (plaster), pp. 38 and 71 (bronze). Kirstein 1946b, pp. 1, 15. Gardner 1965, p. 15. W82, pp. 356–75.

The date of *Fighting Lions* is based on its formal and thematic similarities to the *Dying Centaur* (cat. 6) and to two works from 1871, the lost painting *Lion and Snake* and the drawing *Lion and Mouse* (ill. 19). The treatment of the lion's mane bears a striking resemblance as well to the hair in a bust of *Mary Fay* (Estate of Alvin F. Schmidt, Hardy, Ark.; replicas in a private collection in Jackson, N.H., and at Chesterwood, Stockbridge, Mass.), which Rimmer sculpted with Daniel Chester French during the winter of 1871–72. The dimensions, form, and theme of *Fighting Lions* suggest its placement between the overpowering *Dying Centaur* and the more sedate *Mary Fay*.

A number of drawings can be related to *Fighting Lions*. The drawing from the Bates Sketchbook lacks the more concentrated power of the later sculpture, but is similar in theme, form, and features. The three groups of wrestling lions in the lost drawing may represent a further investigation of the form developed in the sketchbook work, and are similar in form to the sculpture. Although these drawings do not necessarily qualify as preparatory ones, they show Rimmer working out an idea that would eventually culminate in the sculpture.

In theme and treatment *Fighting Lions* evokes the mythic reservoir from which Rimmer constantly drew and in particular the concerns expressed in the *Dying Centaur*. The *Centaur* portrays the profound sympathy between man's animal and human aspects, *Fighting Lions* the eternal struggle between the masculine and feminine natures present in every human being. Sexual imagery in *Fighting Lions* is powerful, even violent.

It may seem at first that the male lion has dominated the female. But the work's form suggests otherwise: the two animals are conceived as one mass, physically and formally interlocked to create an entity of surging power. The stump, to the right of the heads, is so skillfully merged with the animals that it too assumes an expressive strength of its own. Its roots suggest grasping claws. The tightly packed forms are shaped into a pyramidal mass whose apex is formed by the mane. Within this structure, naturalistic anatomy and animated surface texture convey a feeling of concentrated energy. As in the *Falling Gladiator* (cat. 5) and the *Dying Centaur*, a compositional spiral acts as a formal expression of the chosen theme, the integration of ostensibly irreconcilable forces.

The anthropomorphic expression of rage on the male lion's face demonstrates the affinity Rimmer felt between the animal and the human, which he was able to convey by what might be called his romantic empathy. The beasts in *Fighting Lions*, although clearly based on naturalistic observation, exhibit an expressionistic flair that Rimmer could also have found in other works of art. There is an affinity with lions by Géricault and Delacroix, and most importantly with the ferocious realism of the animals by Barye.

Rimmer's two works from 1871, his lost painting *Lion and Snake* and the surviving drawing *Lion and Mouse*, both have compositional affinities with Barye's well-known 1832 sculpture *Lion Crushing a Serpent*, which was familiar to Rimmer at least in an engraving. Rimmer's three-dimensional rendering of lions, more turbulent than his depictions of them in paintings and drawings, approaches the combative realism and aggressive energy of Barye. Both artists depict violent action, but where Barye's forms remain discrete entities, Rimmer unites the two creatures into one writhing mass.

8. Torso
1877

Plaster, 11¼ × 16½ × 7¾ in. (28.60 × 41.93 × 19.70 cm). Signed and dated, on top of base, at the front: W. Rimmer 1877.

Museum of Fine Arts, Boston, 19.128. Acquired on July 17, 1919, as bequest of CHR.

Provenance. CHR.

Exhibitions. 1916: MFA.

Bibliography. Feb. 10, 1917: will of CHR, Article IX. Craven 1968, p. 355. Nov. – Dec. 1976: H. W. Janson, "The Trouble with American Nineteenth Century Sculpture," *American Art Review,* ill. p. 54. W82, pp. 387–90.

Torso is the only sculpture created by Rimmer after his disappointment over the 1875 commission for a plaster statue of *Faith* (whereabouts unknown), which was intended as a model for the figure atop the *National Monument to the Forefathers* at Plymouth. Another sculptor altered Rimmer's model so much that the final statue can hardly be considered his work. *Torso* is powerful, though small in size, and unusual in that it bears a date. The strong emphasis on anatomy and the Classical and Renaissance style suggest that it was modeled as an instructional piece for Rimmer's classes at the School of the Museum of Fine Arts, which had begun in January 1877. Given the right creative environment, Rimmer could still produce sculpture of high quality.

Possible sources for *Torso* include the *Illissos* from the Elgin marbles, which Rimmer admired and often drew during his lectures on art anatomy; the *Torso Belvedere*; and Michelangelo's *Adam* from the Sistine Chapel. The absence of genitals is typical of Rimmer's work; nevertheless the work possesses a certain erotic power.

Although *Torso* shows a debt to the past, it also looks to the future. Its emphasis on expressive form rather than on literary content marks it as a prophetic work. The reliance on the eloquence of the human body places *Torso* on an artistic level above the work of Rimmer's contemporaries and anticipates Rodin's modern vision.

Torso has many affinities with Rimmer's early masterpiece *Seated Man* (cat. 2), of nearly fifty years before. Both are small in size but powerful in impact. In *Seated Man* form acts as a vehicle for private meaning, whereas in *Torso* it is investigated more for its own sake. The differences, however, are more a matter of degree than of kind, more a matter of the image presented than of the way that image is achieved. *Seated Man* looks forward to the concerns embodied in *Torso. Torso* seems a fitting work to end Rimmer's sculptural *oeuvre,* for though it certainly partakes of its own time, it has a simplicity and power that are definitely modern.

PAINTINGS

9. Ebenezer K. Alden

c. 1841–c. 1846

Oil on canvas, 36 × 30 in. (91.45 × 76.20 cm)

Mead Art Museum, Amherst College, Amherst, Mass., 1934.4. Gift of Mrs. Allston Sinnott, Bridgewater, Mass.; presented by Professor Edmund K. Alden, Amherst 1880, at Commencement, 1934.

Provenance. The sitter; later his granddaughter, Mrs. Allston Sinnott.

Bibliography. W82, pp. 413–21.

Most of Rimmer's portraits were done during the 1840's and depict friends or acquaintances from Randolph and its vicinity. Although he customarily followed a compositional formula and used a subdued palette, he often demonstrated an acute grasp of his sitters' character. The nature of the commission seems to have dictated the size and complexity of each work, for some are rather sparse and others more elaborate (see below and cat. 14).

Some of the portraits done during the 1840's, like *Ebenezer K. Alden* and *Reverend Calvin Hitchcock* (Fogg Art Museum, Harvard University), exhibit certain anatomical anomalies that are seemingly inexplicable in light of Rimmer's sound and expert knowledge of human anatomy. In the Hitchcock portrait, we find a swollen body too large for the head, and in both works shoulders are treated disproportionately.

The contrast between competent portrayal of the features and awkward rendering of the body occurs frequently in Rimmer's paintings and lithographs but is absent from his work in other media. He seems to have been better able to render anatomical features in the more tactile plastic medium of sculpture, in the more immediate medium of drawing, and in his paintings of nude figures unencumbered by clothes. Such incongruities become less discernible in his portraits from the 1850's onwards. But although his later portraits are more sophisticated, they never completely break away from the compositional elements of the earlier portraits.

All Rimmer's portraits exhibit a certain plastic strength, suggesting that his sculptural approach to human form may provide a partial explanation for their anatomical shortcomings. This plasticity is particularly evident in his mature portrait of *Mrs. Robert Restiaux Kent* (cat. 23) from 1867. A friend of Rimmer's, Mrs. Kent was the daughter of Captain Horace Howard Watson, whose portrait Rimmer had painted in the 1860's (private collection, Walnut Creek, Calif.) and whose family had ties to royalist émigrés. In the Kent portrait, Rimmer has deemphasized the sitter's rather large nose by the use of lighting and the placement of the head. Similarly in the Alden portrait Rimmer used contrasts of light and shadow and the accentuation of eyebrows and hair to present an image of virility.

A compositionally related but stylistically dissimilar work is Rimmer's 1868 *Young Woman* (cat. 25), which may be the portrait of a living woman or a more idealized work. The woman's features and a similar hat appear in a related drawing, but her features and hat may also derive in part from a popular image of Flora MacIvor that appears in the Rimmer Album (Boston Medical Library). The distraught and even tormented features of *Young Woman*, as well as the somewhat mysterious and unsettling ambiance, make the identification of this subject problematical.

Rimmer's last known portrait, also titled *Young Woman* (cat. 32), may be of his youngest daughter, Caroline Hunt Rimmer. Although generally related in composition and style to his other portraits, it is more atmospheric and may reflect the influence of William Morris Hunt's work. The face of Rimmer's sitter is mature, strong, and thoughtful. By the use of costume, coiffure, anatomy, and subtle tonality he created a delicate and sensitive portrayal. Although Rimmer did use his children's features in a number of his works from the 1840's and 1850's (see *Juliet and the Nurse*, cat. 20 and *Massacre of the Innocents*, cat. 21), if this portrait is in fact of Caroline Hunt Rimmer, it is his only actual portrait of one of his children.

Compared to Rimmer's other portraits, his 1841 *Portrait of a Young Man* (cat. 10) is rather elaborate. It is also Rimmer's earliest known dated painting. Although the identity of the sitter is not known, his sense of self-importance is emphasized by pose, rich costume, items on the desk, and a rather pretentious background suggesting a landscape or a stage set. The verso inscription in Latin may also reflect the importance of this commission. The sitter's grasping personality is subtly expressed by stubby, almost bestial hands, a corpulent body, and an open-armed pose. This elaborate composition is unique among Rimmer's portraits, probably because his other sitters were less affluent as well as because he found it more practical and economical to rely on a compositional formula.

Some of Rimmer's most memorable portraits are of self-made men, represented here by his portrait of *Colonel Seth Turner* (cat. 12), which Turner family tradition relates was painted just before the sitter's death on October 2, 1842. Rimmer has captured a deathlike pallor in this painting and presented us with a veritable "presence." He seems to have admired men like Colonel Turner, Captain Watson, and Abel Kingman who had made long and successful lives for themselves. Perhaps he was drawn to them because their lives were in such stark contrast to his father's.

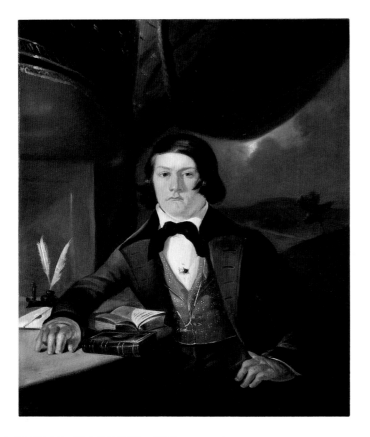

11. The Flower of the Forest
1841

Oil on canvas, 21 × 14 in. (53.33 × 35.55 cm).
Signed and inscribed, at the bottom: The Flower of the
Forest–by W. Rimmer.

Mrs. S. [Seth] T. [Turner] Crawford. Turner family
inheritance.

Provenance. Mr. and Mrs. Royal Turner, Randolph,
Mass. Inherited by their son Seth and left to his daugh-
ter Ellen Turner Crawford; then to her son Seth Turner
Crawford, and on his death to his widow.

Bibliography. W82, pp. 424–26.

Stylistically related to the 1841 *Portrait of a
Young Man* (cat. 10), this painting may have
been intended as a marriage portrait of Rimmer's
young bride. It was not unusual for Rimmer to
give away works with personal meaning, other
examples being his paintings *Hagar and Ishmael*
(ill. 6) and *Flight and Pursuit* (cat. 29).

10. Portrait of a Young Man
1841

Oil on canvas, 36½ × 29½ in. (92.70 × 74.93 cm).
Signed, inscribed, and dated, on back of the canvas:
W. Rimmer/Pinxt/1841. Inscribed (stamped/sten-
ciled), on back of canvas, in lower right corner (in
upper right corner relative to position of the signature,
etc.): CANVAS, COLORS, & C. [i.e., "etc."]/PREPARED
BY/COTTON & LIVELY/13 TREMONT ROW, BOSTON.

Foxborough Historical Society, Foxborough, Mass. Received from Mr. David Bragg in the early 1960's, when
the Historical Society was reorganized.

Provenance. The first owner was the sitter (identity unknown). The next known owner was the first Foxborough Historical Society, which was dissolved in the
early 1900's; on its dissolution the painting was en-
trusted to a Dr. Bragg of Foxborough, who bequeathed
it to his son David.

Bibliography. W82, pp. 421–23.

For discussion, see cat. 9.

12. Colonel Seth Turner
1842

Oil on canvas, 36 × 29⅛ in. (91.45 × 74.00 cm).
Inscribed and signed, on label on back: Nov 15 1756–
Oct 2, 1842/painted by Wm Rimmer.

Mrs. S. T. Crawford. Since 1979 the painting has been
on temporary loan to the Massachusetts Historical Society, Boston.

Provenance. Mr. and Mrs. Royal Turner, Randolph,
Mass. (Royal Turner was the son of Colonel Seth
Turner and married Maria White.) For subsequent own-
ers, see Provenance for *Flower of the Forest*, cat. 11.)

Bibliography. W82, pp. 429–31.

For discussion, see cat. 9.

13. Henry VIII and Anne Boleyn(?)
1844–c. 1848

Oil on canvas, 24 × 20 in. (60.95 × 50.80 cm).
Signed, in pencil, on top piece of stretcher: W.
RimmeR. Signed, in pencil, on bottom piece of
stretcher: W. RimmeR. Inscribed (stamped/stenciled),
on back of canvas, upper left corner (upside down in
relation to recto image): PREPARED BY/MORRIS/N°.
28/EXCHANGE St./BOSTON. Inscribed, on top piece of
stretcher, above the signature: 20 × 24.

Brigham Young University Art Museum Collection,
Provo, Utah. Gift of C. Joseph Bowdring in the memory of his friend John Castano, Dec. 11, 1980.

Provenance. Horatio Lamb family, Milton, Mass. Sold
c. 1955 to John Castano, Boston and Needham
Heights. Sold in 1976 to C. Joseph Bowdring. For a
varient provenance, see W82, p. 439.

Bibliography. W82, pp. 439–42.

The date for this painting can be established on
stylistic evidence and from the canvas seller's
stamp, but the identification of the subject is
more difficult. The painting may represent
Rimmer's first known theater-related work; although the precise incident depicted is not found
in any known plays, a close possibility would be
Act I, Scene IV, of *The Life of Henry the Eighth*
by Shakespeare, in which Henry dances with
Anne Boleyn (there spelled Bullen). An hourglass and music are mentioned in this scene, and
in Rimmer's painting the woman holds a musical instrument and an hourglass rests on a table
at the far right. The subject as presented here is
not found in any illustrations of Shakespeare,
such as those by Boydell, that would have been
available to Rimmer.

Rimmer's reasons for painting this subject are
not known, but the picture is thoughtfully conceived and executed. The figures, the attention
to detail, and the color are particularly impressive. And though Rimmer may have used
images of Henry as a model for the figure, he
may also have borrowed the features of his friend
Abel Kingman, the father of the man with
whom he had studied medicine. Rimmer often
used the features of family members in his
works, especially during the 1840's and 1850's,
and may also have used his friends as models.

14. Mrs. Howland
1846

Oil on canvas, 30⅛ × 24⅝ (76.50 × 62.55 cm).
Inscribed, signed, and dated, on torn label formerly on
back of canvas: Painted by William Rimmer of Boston
1846. Dated, on spine of book held by sitter: 1846.

Private Collection. Bought in 1958 from Miss Mary
Otis of the Mary Otis Antique Shop, East Harwich,
Mass.

Provenance. Dr. and Mrs. Howland left the painting
to their descendants in Fall River, Mass. It was sold
c. 1940 from the Howland House in Fall River to an
antique dealer in Hingham, Mass., who sold it to the
Mary Otis Antique Shop.

Bibliography. W82, pp. 447–49.

For discussion, see cat. 9.

15. Madonna and Child
c. 1847

Oil on canvas, 50 × 40 in. (127.00 × 101.60 cm).
Inscribed, on verso of canvas, in blue crayon, underlined: Miss Rimmer's. Inscribed, in pencil, on the
stretcher: Madonna & Child unfinished, painted by
Dr. William Rimmer. Label, on the stretcher, has
printed "MFA" and written in ink "Dr. Rimmer."

Private Collection. Bought in 1984 from Vose Galleries, Boston.

Provenance. CHR; later an unidentified New Hampshire owner, who sold the painting through an agent in
1981 to Vose Galleries.

Bibliography. W82, pp. 725–28.

For discussion, see cat. 31.

16. Scene from "The Tempest"

c. 1849

Oil on canvas, 36 × 26 in. (91.45 × 66.04 cm). Inscribed (stamped/stenciled), on back of original, unrelined canvas: PREPARED BY/MORRIS/N° 17/Exchange St./BOSTON. (The "17" is handwritten.) Label, on stretcher, now covered by relining, with name of former owner: Brundidge.

Joseph Feldman, Michigan. Bought from a private collector in 1984.

Provenance. Private collection, house on Mission Hill, Milton, Mass. Sold c. 1916 to a Mrs. Brundidge of Milton or a Mrs. Bundidge of Hyde Park, close to Milton. Acquired by Adelson Gallery, Boston. Bought by Ira Spanierman, NYC, and sold in September 1966 to the Drawing Shop—Galerie (Osten-Kaschey), now Shepherd Gallery, Associates, NYC. Acquired in late 1966 by Kennedy Galleries, NYC. Sold to Richard Manoogian, Detroit. Back to Kennedy Galleries, and in 1984 back to Shepherd Gallery, Associates. Sold to a private collector.

Exhibitions. June 9–July 30, 1967: Montreal Museum of Fine Arts, *The Painter and the New World,* 211 (ill.). Sept. 27–Oct. 14, 1967: Marlborough-Gerson Gallery, NYC, *The New York Painter. A Century of Teaching: Morse to Hoffman,* 95 (ill.). Apr. 9–May 12, 1968: Cincinnati Art Museum, *American Paintings on the Market Today,* 3.

Bibliography. Mar. 1967: *KQ* [Kennedy Quarterly], pp. 38–39. 1978: Brian Arnott, "Fantastic Shakespeare," essay in exhibition catalog of the same title, The Gallery—Stratford, Ontario, p. 4. W82, pp. 465–76.

Scene from "The Tempest," depicting Prospero and Miranda before his cell from Act I, Scene II, with the addition of Caliban, and *Scene from "Macbeth"* (cat. 17), from Act III, Scene V, showing the three witches and their Queen, Hecate, can be dated c. 1849 on stylistic evidence as well as from the canvas seller's stamp on the back of each canvas. Visually exciting and historically important, these paintings exemplify Rimmer's lifelong preoccupation with theatrical subjects, especially Shakespearean themes, and with the theater as an arena of transformation.

In addition to their impressive visual qualities, the paintings also function on a symbolic level as references to the theme of usurped rulership— Prospero's legitimate title was taken from him by

intrigue, Macbeth treasonably overthrew the rightful King—and the contrast of good and evil in the forms of white and black magicians. Rimmer's own role of physician-healer and artist-transformer is embodied in Prospero, the arch-magus who works in harmony with nature to reveal its meaning, as opposed to black magicians like Hecate, who work against nature's laws.

Rimmer's symbolic identification with Prospero offers insights into his own beliefs. At the end of the 1840's, when his father's health was rapidly deteriorating, he was beginning to assume, as firstborn male heir, the full burdens of both the Dauphin myth and his own self-definition. The magical power of symbolic images as mediators of knowledge and as creators of living meaning can be seen throughout Rimmer's work.

17. Scene from "Macbeth"

c. 1849

Oil on canvas, 36 × 26 in. (91.45 × 66.04 cm).
Inscribed (stamped/stenciled), on back of original, unrelined canvas: PREPARED BY/MORRIS/N°. 17/Exchange
St./BOSTON. (The "17" is handwritten.) Label, on
stretcher, now covered by relining, with name of former owner: Brundidge.

Joseph Feldman, Michigan. Bought from a private collector in 1984.

Provenance. Same as for *Scene from "The Tempest"*
(cat. 16), except that this painting was never owned by
Richard Manoogian.

Exhibitions. June 9–July 30, 1967: Montreal Museum
of Fine Arts, *The Painter and the New World*, 212.

Bibliography. March, 1967: *KQ* [Kennedy Quarterly],
pp. 38–39. 1970: James Thomas Flexner, *Nineteenth
Century American Painting*, ill. p. 202; captioned
as "Scene from the Tempest (Macbeth)." W82,
pp. 465–76.

For discussion, see cat. 16.

18. Child Leading Man

c. 1853–1858

Oil on canvas, 22 × 27 in. (55.90 × 68.58 cm).
Signed, lower left: W. Rimmer.

Samuel J. Stein, M.D. Purchased from an unidentified person in 1971.

Provenance. Unidentified collection, NYC; later another unidentified collection.

Exhibition. Perhaps 1883: Chase, 89, as "Samson and Child. Painted about 1854."

Bibliography. W82, pp. 482–84.

Child Leading Man is one of Rimmer's most elaborate history paintings. If the painting is the work exhibited in 1883 as *Samson and Child*, it may recount the incident in Judges 14:16 in which the blind Samson is led from the prison house to be bound between two pillars and asks a child to help him place his hands on these pillars. Although the biblical text does not mention the child leading Samson, the poses suggest that the man is blind and thus identifiable as Samson. In Rimmer's painting the child's somewhat histrionic gesture would appear to be intended for the viewer, not for Samson.

Child Leading Man is related to another picture by Rimmer from around the same time, *Horses at Fountain* (cat. 19). Both titles describe the action in the paintings only superficially. Even if we assume the subject to be Samson, the scene remains enigmatic. *Child Leading Man* has a quality of solemnity, despite the conflagration in the background, which is reinforced by restrained color scheme. As with many of Rimmer's other paintings, *Child Leading Man* eludes allegorical interpretation. It catches our imagination through understatement and remains symbolic.

The child's gesture may also allude to Christian legend—Christ as the soul's guide—or to the Greek god Hermes. Such themes would have been available to Rimmer through Romantic and Transcendentalist sources, and his own work, such as *Scene from "The Tempest"* (cat. 16), shows him to have been open to such multileveled approaches. *Child Leading Man* could

also be seen on a personal level, for the child resembles other children in Rimmer's work of the period—notably the lost *Infant St. Peter, Massacre of the Innocents* (cat. 21), and to a lesser degree the unfinished *Madonna and Child* (cat. 15)—and thus may be modeled after one of his own children.

In composition *Child Leading Man* is related to Rimmer's painting *Juliet and the Nurse* (cat. 20); both have an open right side, a nocturnal setting with a fiery background, and a processional arrangement of figures. With a composition that resembles a stage set, *Child Leading Man* may be another of Rimmer's theater-related works, perhaps deriving from a specific source or performance.

19. Horses at Fountain
1856 and 1857

Oil on canvas, 8¼ × 10 in. (20.95 × 25.40 cm).
Signed and dated, lower right corner: W Rimmer/1856.
Dated and signed, lower left: 1857. W Rimmer. In-
scribed, on top of stretcher, in pencil: C. H. Rimmer.
Label, on bottom piece of stretcher, is inscribed, in
pencil: Horses at/Fountain/Painted by/Wm. Rimmer.

The Art Institute of Chicago, 1975.583. Gift of Mrs.
Eugene A. Davidson, 1975.

Provenance. CHR. Later in a private collection in
Hingham, Mass., from which it was acquired by Uni-
corn Antiques (Anne Brennan, owner) in Hingham.
Sold to Peter Williams of Hingham and by him to
Vose Galleries, Boston, which sold it to Mrs. Eugene A.
Davidson.

Exhibition. Perhaps 1880: MFA, 13.

Bibliography. Mar.–Apr. 1977: Milo M. Naeve, "A
Picture and Sculpture by William Rimmer," *Bulletin of
The Art Institute of Chicago*, pp. 16, 17, 19. Weidman
1983, pp. 147–49, 160–61. W82, 489–93.

Horses at Fountain is unique in Rimmer's *oeuvre*
for bearing both two signatures and two dates on
the recto surface. The painting's small size might
suggest that it was intended as a study for a contemplated larger work, but the finished condition
and double signature and date argue against this
possibility. It is a fully realized, self-contained
artistic statement.

On close examination this seemingly straightforward scene takes on a mysterious character.
The cause of the horses' anxiety is not readily
apparent, and the lithesome figures engaged in
unspecified but frenetic action combine with the
transitional time of day to create an unsettling
ambiance. Above all, the fountain—a provocative combination of architectural elements,
Roman crosses, winged genii, and demonic,
gargoyle-like creatures—creates a disturbing image. It appears to be Rimmer's own creation, and

none of the other monuments in his other work
presents any image like this unsettling architectural assemblage.

The power that emanates from *Horses at
Fountain* is due in part to its understatement
and enigmatic imagery. A hallmark of his finest
paintings, this suggestive quality will be seen
again in a related work of twenty years later,
Sunset/Contemplation (cat. 36).

Exhibitions. 1880: MFA, 19. 1883: Chase, 86.
1946/47: Whitney/MFA, 20. Feb. 13–Mar. 27, 1966:
Denver Art Museum, *Great Stories in Art.* Mar.
1–29, 1968: Boston University School of Fine and
Applied Arts, *Boston Painters 1720–1940*, 67.

Bibliography. 1955: Bartlett H. Hayes, Jr., *The Naked
Truth and Personal Vision*, pp. 69, 71. 1978: Lewis A.
Shepard and David Paley, *American Art at Amherst: A
Summary Catalogue of the Collection at the Mead Art
Gallery, Amherst College*, p. 177. W82, pp. 494–505.

Juliet and the Nurse and *Massacre of the Innocents* (cat. 21) are the second known pair of thematically related paintings by Rimmer, the first
being his *Scene from "The Tempest"* and *Scene
from "Macbeth"* of nearly ten years earlier. This
second pair of companion works treats the theme
of lost innocence: by volition in *Juliet and the
Nurse*, by force in *Massacre of the Innocents*.
Composition, lighting, tonality, and figures are
contrasted toward the variations on this mutual
theme.

For example, the composition of *Juliet and
the Nurse* is relatively open and fluid, with the
three figures arranged in no overt underlying
pattern. Although the right side in each painting
is open, the architectural forms in *Massacre of
the Innocents* are sharply articulated and delineated. The figures are tightly organized by an underlying pyramidal structure, the edges of which
are forcefully delineated by sharp diagonals
within the figural grouping. Also, owing to the
vantage point chosen, the figures are pushed
more into our space than the figures in *Juliet
and the Nurse*.

The lighting in each work is strikingly contrasted. Both pictures share a fiery background,
but almost the entire scene of *Juliet and the
Nurse* is in shadow. Juliet is embraced by an area
of warm, protective light that falls in a pool at
her feet. The light source is as mysterious as the
figure herself, her companions, and the entire
nocturnal setting. By comparison, the light in
Massacre of the Innocents is harsh and cold, ac-
centuating forms and throwing the violent scene
into sharp focus. The light from an unknown
source falls on the foreground woman and her
child in an isolating manner. In *Juliet and the
Nurse* light protects; in *Massacre of the Innocents*
it exposes.

20. Juliet and the Nurse
1857

Oil on canvas, 27 × 22 in. (68.58 × 55.90 cm).
Signed and dated, lower right corner: W. Rimmer
1857. Signed and inscribed, before removal during
1968 restoration, lower right corner: W. Rimmer. /
Pinxt.

The Addison Gallery of American Art, Phillips Academy, Andover, Mass., 1952.2. Gift of Lincoln Kirstein, 1952.

Provenance. Rimmer family, principally CHR. Acquired by Lincoln Kirstein, NYC, who gave it to the
Whitney Museum of American Art, NYC, on May 1,
1947. It was returned to Kirstein in 1949, owing to an
accession policy change at the Whitney.

In both paintings Rimmer has imaginatively presented scenes that do not exist specifically in his textual sources. In *Massacre of the Innocents* he is relatively traditional, encapsulating the event foretold in Matthew 2:16 and concentrating essentially on one dramatic, symbolic event. His rendition of *Juliet and the Nurse* is more imaginative. Juliet, her nurse, and her attendant Peter seem to be on their way to Juliet's wedding, an event that takes place offstage between Scenes V and VI of Act II of Shakespeare's *Romeo and Juliet*. Rimmer's depiction of Juliet's nurse is faithful to Mercutio's description of her as ugly (Act II, Scene IV, lines 113–14), but it is his apparent borrowing from Leonardo for this woman's face that is particularly striking. How Rimmer knew Leonardo's drawing of the so-called "Ugly Duchess" is uncertain; perhaps he had come across a print of it in pursuing his anatomical studies through the byways of typology, phrenology, and physiognomy. The figures of Juliet, Peter, and her nurse may allude to the Ages of Man, and the borrowing from Leonardo would fit this symbolic context.

Juliet's features may derive from those of Rimmer's three surviving daughters. The figure type may be based on the work of Gerard Dou or on commercial images that appear in the Rimmer Album (Boston Medical Library). The mysterious ambiance with which this painting is imbued may be informed by Rimmer's interest in and sensitivity to Spiritualism.

Both *Juliet and the Nurse* and *Massacre of the Innocents* present themes that find possible covert meaning in Rimmer's own life, which was especially desperate during the 1850's. Specifically, the child in *Massacre of the Innocents* may be modeled on Rimmer's last-born son, Horace, 1857–59. The painting may represent Rimmer's worst fears about his last male heir's fragility in light of the early deaths of four of the eight Rimmer children born during the 1840's and 1850's. This is also one level of meaning for Rimmer's painting *Hagar and Ishmael* (ill. 6), from the same time.

21. Massacre of the Innocents
c. 1858

Oil on canvas, 27 × 22 in. (68.58 × 55.90 cm).
Signed, lower right: W. Rimmer.

Mead Art Gallery, Amherst College, Amherst, Mass., 1974.92. Gift of Herbert W. Plimpton, 1974, in honor of his father, Hollis W. Plimpton '15.

Provenance. Owned by a Dr. Holmes of Milton, Mass. Acquired by an unidentified prominent Boston family. Sold in 1958 to a local dealer, Charlotte Webster, of Boston, who sold it the same year to Vose Galleries, Boston. Sold on Feb. 1, 1961, to James Graham & Sons, NYC, who sold it in April 1967 to Herbert W. Plimpton. It was in the Herbert W. Plimpton Collection at Amherst College from 1967 to 1974.

Exhibition. June 1972–Apr. 1973: University Art Museum, Berkeley; National Collection of Fine Arts, Washington; Dallas Museum of Fine Arts; and Indianapolis Museum of Art, *The Hand and the Spirit: Religious Art in America 1700–1900*, 89.

Bibliography. Bartlett 1882, pp. 35–36. 1978: Shepard and Paley, *American Art at Amherst* (see cat. 20 Bibliography), p. 177. W82, pp. 495–505.

For discussion, see cat. 20.

ILL. 6. *Hagar and Ishmael.*

Hagar and Ishmael (ill. 6)

c. 1858

Oil on canvas, 30 × 25 in. (76.20 × 63.50 cm).
Courtesy of Lee Anderson.

Like *Massacre of the Innocents* (cat. 21), this painting alludes to the tragic fragility of children's lives in Rimmer's time. Rimmer's son Horace, died in 1859. Hagar strongly resembles Rimmer's wife Mary, and the faces of children in other works of his, such as the unfinished *Madonna and Child* (cat. 15) and *Child Leading Man* (cat. 18), are believed to be modeled after those of his own children. To varying degrees these works exemplify Rimmer's way of alluding symbolically in his art to profoundly personal experiences. *Hagar and Ishmael* may not actually refer to Horace's death but to a severe illness, since the scene depicted, Genesis 21:14–16, implies the resuscitation of Ishmael. Rimmer's lurid color scheme makes a fine complement to Hagar's emotions of grief and despair.

22. A Riderless War Horse

c. 1865–1870

Oil on canvas, 34 × 28 in. (86.37 × 71.12 cm)

Clarence and Mildred Long. Bought in 1975 from Vose Galleries, Boston.

Provenance. The artist. Later owned by various unidentified private collectors. Acquired by James McGrath, private dealer from Winchester, Mass., and sold to Vose Galleries.

Related work. Pencil drawing *Horse*, Fogg Art Museum, Harvard University, 1936.10.11. See W82, p. 822.

Exhibitions. Feb. 1–Mar. 4, 1962: MFA, *The Civil War: The Artist's Record*, 3882, lent by Vose Galleries. Sept.–Oct. 1962: Washington County Museum of Fine Arts, Hagerstown, Md., *Civil War Centennial Exhibition*, *1862–1962*, 42 (section on Oil Paintings). Nov. 1971–early June 1972: Didier's (antique shop), New Orleans, La.

Bibliography. W82, pp. 515–19.

For discussion, see cat. 26.

23. Mrs. Robert Restiaux Kent
1867

Oil on canvas, 30 × 25 in. (76.20 × 63.50 cm)

Museum of Fine Arts, Boston, 49.27. Gift of Mrs. Richard B. Kent, 1949, in the name of Henry Watson Kent.

Provenance. First owned by the sitter, née Eliza F. Watson, and her husband, Robert Restiaux Kent. Given to their son Henry Watson Kent, NYC; owned after his death in 1948 by Mrs. Richard B. Kent.

Exhibitions. 1946/47: Whitney/MFA, 11 (ill.). Nov. 11–26, 1955: Boston Symphony Orchestra, *Seventy-five Years of Painting in Boston*, with title "Woman at the Piano."

Bibliography. Nov. 11, 1955: "Symphonia 75 Years of Painting in Boston," *Fifth Program, Concert Bulletin, Boston Symphony Orchestra*, pp. 215, 216. 1969: *American Paintings in the Museum of Fine Arts, Boston*, Vol. I, 829, p. 215. W82, pp. 534–37.

For discussion, see cat. 9.

24. Scene from "Romeo and Juliet"
1867–1868

Oil on canvas, 12¹⁵⁄₁₆ × 15¹⁵⁄₁₆ in. (32.90 × 40.50cm). Signed and dated, lower right corner: W. Rimmer 1867–8.

The University of Michigan Museum of Art, The Paul Leroy Grigaut Memorial Collection, 1969.2.82. Acquired in 1969 from the estate of Paul L. Grigaut.

Provenance. Castano Galleries, Boston. Sold to Paul L. Grigaut.

Related work. Pencil sketch *Head of an Old Man* (Detroit Institute of Arts, 69.474), related to man in left side of painting. See W82, pp. 897–99.

Exhibitions. 1946/47: Whitney/MFA, 13, lent by Paul L. Grigaut. Apr. 10–May 6, 1962: Detroit Institute of Arts, *American Paintings and Drawings from Michigan Collections*, 42 (ill.). Sept. 14–Oct. 12, 1969: U. of Michigan Museum of Art, *A Connoisseur's Choice: From the Collection of Paul L. Grigaut*, 51. June 5–July 23, 1978: The Gallery–Stratford, Ontario, *Fantastic Shakespeare*, 51, as "Closing Scene from King Lear."

Bibliography: W82, pp. 537–43.

The painting I have called *Scene from "Romeo and Juliet"* has also been tentatively identified as depicting the closing scene from *King Lear*, but Rimmer's details are inconsistent with those of that scene; nor is *King Lear*'s theme of enobling suffering apparent in the painting.

As suggested by Lincoln Kirstein, *Romeo and Juliet* seems a more likely source. Although the locale is not a city, the figures and the dramatic confrontation of the two groups aptly fit the action in Act III, Scene I, of *Romeo and Juliet*, in which the Montagues and the Capulets arrive to find the slain bodies of Mercutio and Tybalt, both killed as a result of Romeo's actions. We should also remember that this episode was followed by Romeo's banishment, and that the theme of exile was one that held deep personal meaning for Rimmer.

Whether or not there is a covert meaning to this painting, the setting borrows motifs from the theater and may have been inspired by an actual performance, perhaps of Gounod's opera *Romeo and Juliet*, which was given at the Academy of Music in New York on December 14, 1867. To varying degrees, all Rimmer's theater-related works show familiarity both with the plays themselves and with their performances. The majority of these works are based on Shakespeare's plays, and at least three can be related to *Romeo and Juliet* (see cat. 20, 24, and 30).

25. Young Woman
1868

Oil on academy board, 15¼ × 11¾ in. (38.73 × 29.85 cm). Signed and dated, lower left corner: W. Rimmer/1868. Label, on back of board: Prepared Mill-Board/Winsor & Newton/Artists' Colourmen/To Her Majesty/and to/His Royal Highness Prince Albert/38, Rathbone Place, London. Label, on stretcher, has title: Portrait of a Young Girl.

Morton C. Bradley, Jr. Bought from Fayette Gallery (Irving Barlow, owner), Boston.

Provenance. Castano Galleries, Boston. Sold to Gustave D. Klimann, Boston, and by him to Fayette Gallery.

Related work. Wash drawing in india ink on paper, *Head of a Woman in a Hat* (MFA, 81.109a). See W82, pp. 912–13.

Exhibition. 1946/47: Whitney/MFA, 13, lent by Gustave D. Klimann.

Bibliography. W82, pp. 549–51.

For discussion, see cat. 9.

63

26. Victory
1870/1878–1879

Oil on canvas, 20 × 27 in. (50.80 × 68.58 cm).
Signed, lower right: W. Rimmer. Signed and dated,
below outstretched rear legs of horse: W. Rimmer
1870. (The name is underlined.) Inscribed, on lower
stretcher bar, in partially obliterated (faded) ink: Victory
ar [or "as"; before this appears to be the faded remnants
of an "L" or of an "l" and after the "ar" or "as" appears
to be the top or middle cross bar of a "t"] subject/
painted by W. Rimmer. Label, on back: Museum of
Fine Arts/W. J. Gardner/498 Boylston/no frame 35.
Label, on back: 1818. (This is the shipping number for
1947: MFA.) Label, on back: Paul L. Grigaut, Detroit.

The Detroit Institute of Arts, 69.293. Founders Society
Purchase, 1969, with the Dexter M. Ferry Jr. Fund.
Purchased from the Estate of Paul L. Grigaut.

Provenance. W. J. Gardner, Boston. Later Mr. and
Mrs. William J. Gunn, Newtonville, Mass. Acquired
by Castano Galleries, Boston, and sold in October
1946 to Paul L. Grigaut.

Related work. Drawing *Victory* (cat. 60).

Exhibitions. 1946/47: Whitney/MFA, lent by Paul L.
Grigaut; the painting did not appear in the catalog and
was not assigned a number because it arrived too late.
Apr. 4–May 17, 1959: Corcoran Gallery of Art, Wash-
ington, D.C., *The American Muse*, 67 (ill.). Sept.
14–Oct. 12, 1969: U. of Michigan Museum of Art,
*A Connoisseur's Choice: From the Collection of
Paul L. Grigaut*, 52, lent by the Estate of Paul L.
Grigaut.

Bibliography. 1961: Henri Dorra, *The American Muse*,
p. 97. 1970: James L. Greaves, *Conservation Services
Laboratory Summary of Condition Report*, Detroit Institute of Arts. 1977: Graham Hood, Nancy Rivard,
and Kathleen Pyne, "American Paintings Acquired
During the Last Decade," *Bulletin of the Detroit Institute of Arts*, Vol. 55, No. 2; N.R. (Nancy Rivard) entry
on the painting, pp. 84, 85, 87. W82, pp. 562–70.

Victory and *Civil War Scene* (ill. 7) make up the
third known pair of thematically related paintings in Rimmer's *oeuvre* (see cat. 16 and 17, 20
and 21). Unlike the other paintings, these were
preceded by preparatory drawings. Both paintings contain vivid contrasts of color, emotions,
and themes that point out the irony of death
amidst victory. They are rich in both personal
and universal symbolism. X-ray examination has
revealed a finished painting of a landscape
underneath *Victory*—the only known case of
Rimmer's reusing a canvas. The dating of *Victory* is problematical. Its stretcher inscription
suggests that the painting is Rimmer's last, but
the painting bears the date 1870. The horse is
closer in form to horses in two paintings by
Rimmer from the mid-1870's, *Battle of the
Amazons* (cat. 35) and *To the Charge* (cat. 34),

than to the horse in *Civil War Scene*. The subject matter of *Victory* is the kind that would have interested Rimmer throughout the decade, having at once historical, mythic, and personal levels of meaning.

Victory is one of Rimmer's few pictures for which there is a clearly related drawing (cat. 60). The drawing was not dated by Rimmer, but the subject, if not the dress of the rider, suggests that it is related to the Civil War. Although Truman Bartlett does not include this drawing in an illustrated group of Rimmer's Civil War drawings (*Art Life*, p. 123), its mythic treatment is perfectly in keeping with some of Rimmer's finest studies on that theme, e.g., those from 1867 that allude symbolically to the war by portraying war-related classical subjects (see *A Dead Soldier*, cat. 52). *A Riderless War Horse* (cat. 22) is another kind of allusion to the Civil War, one whose mythic structure extends to embrace the historical content. Whether symbolic of a specific or a general victory or of both, Rimmer's horse and rider in the *Victory* drawing are much less sinister than those in the painting, where by color and by style they have been transformed into a demonic entity.

Rimmer's painting may also allude to Death on a pale horse (Revelation 6). Iconographically Rimmer's theme has a number of well-known precedents, notably Benjamin West's large 1796 painting *Death on the Pale Horse* (Detroit Institute of Arts); but it is not certain that Rimmer knew this image or any of the others. Unlike West, Rimmer concentrates on a single horse and rider isolated against a deep landscape.

Considering *Victory*'s subject and its stretcher inscription, it is also possible to interpret the painting in terms of Rimmer's awareness of his own impending death. This would indicate a date toward the end of the 1870's. Conversely, the work might be related to his increasing difficulties at Cooper Union in 1870. Whatever its date, *Victory* is not easily reducible to any simple interpretation; rather, the painting is infused with various complex themes that have death as a component.

Civil War Scene (ill. 7)
c. 1871

Oil on canvas, 20¼ × 27¼ in. (51.43 × 69.22 cm).
Courtesy of The Detroit Institute of Arts.

The subject of the painting relates it to the Civil War era, but its stylistic affinity with *English Hunting Scene* (ill. 9) of 1871 argues for a date around that time. The composition here is more elaborate than in the preparatory drawing, *Soldier and Horse Under a Tree* (ill. 8), belonging to the Fogg Art Museum. There are also many elements of contrast that suggest both victory and defeat: the wounded man who finds solace in the memories elicited by the image he gazes at; the flowing water and the empty cup; the sunlit landscape and the destruction within it. In the finished work Rimmer transformed the drawing's journalistic image of a soldier in a reflective moment into a commentary on the futility of war and the suffering that must be borne by both sides.

ILL. 8. *Soldier and Horse Under a Tree*, c. 1869–71. Pencil on white ruled paper; 5½ × 7½ in. (14 × 19.05 cm). *Courtesy of the Harvard University Art Museums (Fogg Art Museum).*

ILL. 7. *Civil War Scene.*

27. The Master Builder
c. 1871

Oil and sepia on academy board, 21⅞ × 15⁹⁄₁₆ in.
(55.50 × 39.50 cm). Signed, lower right: W. Rimmer.
Label on back has information regarding the 1916 MFA
exhibition: Loan 151.16 [registration number]/lent by
Miss Susan [Minns].

Leonard and Corrine Lemberg.

Provenance. Miss Susan Minns, Boston. Acquired by
Castano Galleries, Boston, and sold to William W.
Hobé, NYC. Sold to Benjamin Lemberg, Detroit, and
bequeathed to Leonard Lemberg.

Related work. Pencil sketch "Master Builder" on lost
sheet of sketches from c. November 1870; a glass negative from 1916 survives at the MFA. See W82,
pp. 992–93.

Exhibitions. 1880: MFA, 16, lent by Miss Susan
Minns, Boston. 1916: MFA, lent by Miss Susan
Minns. 1946/47: Whitney/MFA, 16, lent by William
W. Hobé, NYC.

Bibliography. Bartlett 1882, p. 127. 1930: H.
Winthrop Pierce, *The History of the School of the Museum of Fine Arts, Boston, 1877–1927*, p. 54. W82,
pp. 576–82.

For discussion, see cat. 33.

English Hunting Scene (ill. 9)
1871

Oil on canvas mounted on board, 48 × 72 in. (121.90
× 182.90 cm). Courtesy of the Museum of Fine Arts,
Boston.

English Hunting Scene—a melange of early-
nineteenth-century English landscape styles
within an Italianate structure, similar to works
by Thomas Cole and Washington Allston—is
Rimmer's largest known painting. Its size and
the fact that it bears little resemblance to a
number of lost landscapes by Rimmer suggest
the possibility that the painting was commissioned. The fashionable subject and bright color
scheme reflect Rimmer's artistic success after his
return to Boston.

ILL. 9. *English Hunting Scene.*

28. Interior/Before the Picture
1872

Oil on academy board, 12 3/16 × 9 1/16 in. (31.13 × 23.50 cm.). Signed (twice) and dated, lower left: W. Rimmer./W. Rimmer/1872. Inscribed, on back, in ink, at the top: Sale 5 # 1. Inscribed, in pencil, on back, in the middle, below previous inscription: Interior/W. Rimmer/1872/(CHR). Drawing *Child's Head* on verso (see W82, pp. 1184–85).

Richard L. Feigen. Bought on May 21, 1981, at auction from Robert W. Skinner, Inc., Bolton, Mass. (agent for Clifford A. Kaye, Brookline, Mass.).

Provenance. CHR; then perhaps ERS. Acquired by Edward R. Morrill, Boston, bookseller, and given to his son Samuel, also a Boston bookseller. Sold in 1970 to Clifford A. Kaye, Brookline, Mass.; auctioned on May 21, 1981 by Robert W. Skinner, Inc.

Exhibitions. Perhaps Feb. 1877: Review Club Exhibition, Chelsea, Mass., as *Contemplation*. Perhaps 1880: MFA, 20 or 23. 1916: MFA, lent by CHR.

Bibliography: 1981: Robert W. Skinner, Inc., *American and European Paintings*, lot (entry) 51. W82, pp. 588–92.

Interior/Before the Picture depicts a contemplative moment set in the midst of a comfortable, richly furnished room. The scene may be Rimmer's home in Chelsea, and the woman may represent his youngest daughter, Caroline Hunt Rimmer, who was a sculptor. Certainly the pieces of sculpture that appear in the painting resemble her work. If it does represent his home and his daughter, this painting would be Rimmer's only known painted domestic scene.

The woman also bears a distinct resemblance to the female types in commercial images printed in the Rimmer Album (Boston Medical Library). Also, although the setting could well be a Victorian parlor from the early 1870's, the woman's costume is not of that time but rather suggests a composite of English and American theater-derived fancy dress of the 1840's and 1850's. This anachronism is enhanced by her pose, which, combined with her dress and fan, suggests reflection before going to or after arriving from a fancy dress ball. Although in this

respect *Interior/Before the Picture* resembles images by contemporary European artists such as James Tissot and Alfred Stevens, the ethereal ambiance, hazy background, and cool colors, together with the woman's pose and her quiet, devotional gaze, suggest some sort of religious import.

Interior/Before the Picture is one of the most intimate pictures done by Rimmer, and like many of his finest works it also possesses an enigmatic and unsettling quality. The atmosphere is hazy and soft, but the woman is somewhat distanced from it by the crisp outline of her form. The decor, especially the right foreground with its heavy sideboard-chest, drapes, and chair, is claustrophobic; compositionally and metaphorically, the room tends to weigh down on the figure.

The elements of solitude, introspection, reverie, and understatement in this painting are also found in another painting of a single woman, Rimmer's later *At the Window* (cat. 30). In *At the Window* we are primarily dealing with an idealized figure, Rimmer's female type, with her classical profile. Also, it is quite likely that *At the Window* depicts a theatrical subject, perhaps the opening of Act II, Scene II, of *Romeo and Juliet*.

29. Flight and Pursuit
1872

Oil on canvas, 18⅛ × 26¼ in. (46.00 × 66.70 cm). Signed and dated, lower right corner: W. Rimmer/1872.

Museum of Fine Arts, Boston, 56.119. Bequest of Miss Edith Nichols, 1956.

Provenance. Given by the artist in late December 1872 to Colonel Charles B. Nichols, Providence, R.I. Colonel Nichols died on October 22, 1877, leaving the painting to his widow, who later gave it to her daughter Edith, of Providence.

Related work. Pencil sketch, *Oh for the Horns of the Altar* (ill. 10), for foreground figure. See W82, pp. 872–78.

Exhibitions. Early Dec. 1872: Williams and Everett's Art Gallery, Boston. Mid–late Dec. 1872: Mr. Brown's gallery, Providence. 1880: MFA, 22. 1946/7: Whitney/MFA, 18 (ill.). Apr. 23–June 9, 1957: Detroit Institute of Arts and M. H. de Young Memorial Museum, San Francisco, *Painting in America, the Story of 450 Years*, 117. Oct. 1, 1959–Oct. 31, 1960: American Federation of Arts, NYC, exhibition number 59–24, circulated in the U.S. as *A Rationale for Modern Art*, 16. May 17–June 18, 1961: Whitney Museum of American Art, *American Painting from 1865–1905*, 52 (ill.). Apr. 16–Sept. 7, 1970: Metropolitan Museum of Art, *19th Century America*, 117 (ill.). Oct. 1–Nov. 17, 1974: Los Angeles County Museum, *American Narrative Painting*, 45 (ill.). Nov. 25, 1980–Aug. 16, 1981: MFA and American Federation of Arts, *The Boston Tradition: American Paintings from the Museum of Fine Arts, Boston*, 51 (entry/catalog by Carol Troyen). Sept. 7, 1983–June 11, 1984: MFA, Corcoran Gallery of Art, Washington, D.C., and Grand Palais, Paris, *A New World: Masterpieces of American Painting 1760–1910*, 76 (ill.), entry by Carol Troyen.

Bibliography. Dec. 8, 1872: "Fine Arts," *Sunday Herald*, Boston. Mid–late Dec. 1872: *Providence Daily Journal*. Bartlett 1882, p. 127; illustrated reversed, corrected in 1970 edition. 1956: E. P. Richardson, *Painting in America*, p. 262. 1966: James Thomas Flexner, *That Wilder Image*, p. 136. 1967: William C. Agee, "Nineteenth-Century Eccentrics and the American Tradition," *The Grand Eccentrics* (Art News Annual XXXII), pp. 149–50. 1969: *American Paintings in the Museum of Fine Arts, Boston*, Vol. I, 831, p. 216. Jan. 1972: Charles A. Sarnoff, M.D., "Symbols in Shadows: A Study of Shadows in Dreams," *Journal of the American Psychoanalytic Association*, pp. 78, 80–81; the ideas are repeated in his "The Meaning of

William Rimmer's *Flight and Pursuit*," *American Art Journal*, May 1973, pp. 18–19. 1976: Jean Lipman and Helen M. Franc, *Bright Stars: American Painting and Sculpture Since 1776*, p. 99. 1976: John Wilmerding, *American Art*, p. 163. June 1976: Marcia Goldberg, "William Rimmer's *Flight and Pursuit*: An Allegory of Assassination," *Art Bulletin*, pp. 234–40. Summer 1981: Ellwood C. Parry III, "Looking for a French and Egyptian Connection Behind William Rimmer's *Flight and Pursuit*," *American Art Journal*, pp. 51–60. W82, pp. 592–626.

Flight and Pursuit is Rimmer's best known but least understood work. A related drawing (ill. 10), which is clearly an initial idea for the foreground figure in the painting, is inscribed "oh for the horns of the Altar." The words, which occur in several Old Testament passages, refer to an ancient practice whereby a murderer could gain asylum by grasping the horns of the altar. Several contemporary reviewers of *Flight and Pursuit* applied the title of the drawing to the painting, and the drawing fits well with this Biblical situation. The steps at the far left as well as the figure's movement, intent stare, and two daggers suggest his goal and reasons for seeking asylum. The painting, with its Near Eastern interior, high steps, and smoke at the far left, reinforces this Biblical theme.

The drawing provides the basic form for the foreground figure in the painting, but the painting's complexity suggests various other visual influences, including works by Gérôme, Doré, and David Scott as well as the works of Italian primitives in the James Jackson Jarves collection at Yale University, which Rimmer could have studied when he lectured at the Yale School of the Fine Arts on February 9, 1872. The silhouetting, template-like quality of Rimmer's figures as well as the atemporal, stop-action quality of the image as a whole may owe something to the works in the Jarves collection.

For the painting's architecture and decoration, Rimmer may have been influenced by paintings depicting Near Eastern architectural subjects, which he would have seen in both Boston and New York. A more likely source was the illustrations of the article "Saracenic Architecture" in *The Iconographic Encyclopedia*, a copy of which

had been given to Rimmer, probably in February 1868, by his pupils at Cooper Union. These illustrations would have provided him with a reference guide for forms that he could also have extracted from paintings but with greater difficulty.

A number of writers have tied *Flight and Pursuit* to the Rimmer family belief that Thomas Rimmer was the disinherited heir to the throne of France. Certainly the action depicted and the title convey feelings of fear and persecution. Because no written notes on the painting by Rimmer himself have come down to us, his specific intentions may never be known. Nonetheless, it is clear that *Flight and Pursuit* is a visual metaphor of some sort, a vehicle for a wide range of symbolic meaning that continues to enthrall viewers and intrigue scholars.

ILL. 10. *Oh, for the Horns of the Altar*, 1867. Pencil on paper; 11⅞ × 14½ in. (30.20 × 36.85 cm). *Courtesy of the Clements C. Fry Print Collection of the Yale Medical Historical Library, Yale University.*

Gladiator and Lion (ill. 11)

1873–1875

Oil on cardboard, 9½ × 12½ in. (24.15 × 31.75 cm). Signed, lower left: Rimmer.

Reynolda House, Winston-Salem, N.C. Deeded in December 1970 by Barbara B. Lassiter. Unavailable for exhibition owing to fragile condition.

Provenance (for other versions see W82, pp. 628–29). The original owner may have been the Rimmer family, principally CHR, or it may have been Mrs. Samuel D. Warren, Boston. Mrs. Warren sold the painting in 1897 to Seth Morton Vose, owner of the Westminster Art Gallery, Providence. He died in 1910, and his stock was inherited by his son Robert of Robert C. Vose Paintings, Boston, which became the Vose Galleries. The painting was sold on Feb. 29, 1944, to Lincoln Kirstein. It was later owned by Robert Isaacson, NYC, and then by Durlacher Brothers, NYC. It was sold in June 1967 to Barbara Babcock Lassiter.

Exhibitions. Jan. 12–Feb. 5, 1876: Boston Art Club, *First Exhibition for 1876*, 91, lent and for sale by the artist. Feb. 14–17, 1877: The Review Club, Chelsea, held in the rooms of the Star of Bethlehem Lodge, Chelsea. Apr. 7–May 1, 1943: Vose Galleries, *The Art of Colonial America and the Early Republic: Primitives, Hudson River School and their Contemporaries*, 43. 1946/47: Whitney/MFA, 26, lent by Lincoln Kirstein. Nov. 27, 1963–Jan. 9, 1964: Minneapolis Institute of Arts, *Four Centuries of American Art*, 27, lent by Durlacher Brothers. July 4–Aug. 16, 1964: California Palace of the Legion of Honor, San Francisco, *American Paintings of the Nineteenth Century*, 67, lent by Durlacher Brothers. Oct. 8–Nov. 2, 1968: The Public Education Association at M. Knoedler and Co., NYC, *The American Vision Paintings, 1825–1875*, 24. Jan. 13–31, 1971: Hirschl & Adler Galleries, NYC, *American Paintings in the Reynolda House Collection*, 18 (ill.).

Bibliography. Feb. 17, 1877: A. H., "Review Club Exhibition," *Chelsea Telegraph and Pioneer*, p. 2. Bartlett 1882, p. 127. Kirstein 1946a, p. 73. W82, pp. 628–646.

This painting is one of Rimmer's most fascinating works. Its dramatic power derives from the kinetic energy embodied in the figures of the two opponents. The lion, ferocious and hypnotic, is caught in the grip of profound pain and rage. One of several depictions of lions by Rimmer (see cat. 7, 56, 66, 77, 78; ill. 17, 19), this creature with a compressed pyramidal form, a huge paw, and mesmerizing features is based on an engraved illustration to an early-nineteenth-century edition of James Ridley's *The Tales of the Genii* (J. Adlard, 1810: Vol I., between pp. 148 and 149; ill. 12). The coincidence of basic image is certainly more than fortuitous, especially since Ridley's tales contain the story of Sadak in search of the waters of oblivion, a subject of one of Rimmer's drawings (see cat. 57). Although Rimmer has reproduced in reverse the pose of the lion in the illustration, his treatment of the

details—flamelike mane, piercing eyes, fore-shortening, and expressive anatomy—has transformed the image.

Rimmer is also indebted to Gérôme's 1859 painting "Ave Caesar! Morituri Te Salutant" (Yale University Art Gallery) for the composition of *Gladiator and Lion*. His familiarity with Gérôme's work is documented by a description of it included in his lecture to a group of students in Providence on February 22, 1873 (reported in "Dr. Rimmer's Ninth Lecture," *Providence Daily Journal*, Feb. 28, 1873, p. 2, column 7). His comments clearly indicate that he and his audience knew either the original painting or one of its variants, rather than simply, for example, its transmission via Thomas Nast's wood engraving *The Tammany Tiger Loose—What are You Going to Do About It?*, which appeared in *Harper's Weekly*, Nov. 11, 1871.

Although undoubtedly inspired by Gérôme's painting, Rimmer did not copy it slavishly. Rather he imaginatively transformed it to fit the size, scale, and symbolic import of his own conception. He compressed the space, essentially reversing the solid-void arrangement of Gérôme's painting, and he omitted Gérôme's archaeological detail. Rimmer's approach to the subject was not predominantly historical, archaeological, or naturalistic; rather he used the material as a vehicle for symbolic content. His gladiator's body type is close to what he considered characteristic of "low types of man" (Bartlett, *Art Life*, p. 103). The helmet and physique relate the figure to the "gladiator type," the lowest level of human being on the phrenological evolutionary scale as expounded by George Combe in his book *Phrenology Applied to Painting and Sculpture* (London: Simpkin, Marshall, and Co., 1855). Excerpts from the book were contained in the February 1860 issue of the *American Phrenological Journal*, an issue that Rimmer possessed.

The phrenological reference and the anthropomorphism of the lion's face imply a moral dimension to Rimmer's painting. Rimmer was fond of depicting noble lions, and his sympathy in this work appears to lie with the lion. However, though the two antagonists stand in opposition to one another, they are united both in composition and by the fact of their conflict. Here again Rimmer returns to the theme of reconciling ostensibly disparate and opposed forces, much as he did in his sculpture *Fighting Lions* (cat. 7).

In fact the two foreground figures are both victims sent into the arena to face death. They are depicted as if frozen, locked in a psychological confrontation as well as a physical one, transformed via solids and voids into a single unit. The gladiator is silhouetted against an open area and the lion against a closed wall, but they share a common dynamism of form and expressive anatomical detail.

30. At the Window
c. 1874–c. 1877

Oil on canvas, 20¼ × 14⅛ in. (51.45 × 35.88 cm). Signed, lower right corner, in black: W. Rimmer. (There is a short line under the two m's.) Label, on back of stretcher, inscribed: Painting— By . William Rimmer/Title–At the Window/Owner—Caroline Hunt Rimmer. Label, on stretcher: FROM/F.C. HASTINGS & CO.,/–IMPORTERS AND DEALERS IN–/ARTISTS' MATERIALS,/54 & 56 Cornhill, near Court St., BOSTON.

National Museum of American Art, Smithsonian Institution, Washington, D.C., 1974.111. Purchased from Post Road Antiques, Larchmont, N.Y., in 1974.

Provenance. CHR, then ERS. Later acquired by Esther Greenwood, Marlborough, Mass., and purchased from her estate by Robert W. Skinner, Inc., Bolton, Mass. Sold at auction to David McCoy, Old Lyme, Conn., and by him to Post Road Antiques.

Exhibitions. Feb. 20–Dec. 4, 1915: San Francisco, *Panama-Pacific International Exposition*, 2692, lent by CHR. 1916: MFA, lent by CHR.

Bibliography. W82, pp. 650–55.

For discussion, see cat. 28.

31. Madonna/Magdalen

c. 1874–c. 1877

Oil on canvas, 60 × 29 in. (152.50 × 73.50 cm).
Signed, lower left: W. Rimmer. Label on back has:
RAYMOND FALLONA, INC./Upholsterers. Decorators/Boston Brookline.

Richard L. Feigen & Co., NYC. Bought at auction on
May 12, 1983, from Robert W. Skinner, Inc., Bolton,
Mass.

Provenance. Found in a shop in Andover, Mass., by an
unidentified person and sold to Robert W. Skinner, Inc.

Related works. Lost crayon drawing, same title (see
W82, pp. 1020–21). Engraving by W. B. Closson (The
Art Museum, Princeton U.), done after the painting;
illustrated in Bartlett 1880, following p. 514.

Bibliography. Bartlett 1880, p. 511. Bartlett 1882,
p. 117. Kirstein 1946*b*, p. 5. May 1983: Robert W.
Skinner, Inc., *An Auction of Fine Paintings*, sale 898,
entry 70 as "Angel." W82, pp. 655–57.

Although the subject is potentially saccharine,
Rimmer avoids bathos by emphasizing the figure's anatomical strength and stability of form.
He may have had this painting in mind when
he said, "instead of making a glory around the
head, I wish to make the whole body a glory"
(Bartlett, *Art Life*, p. 117). The robust quality of
this work is also found in Rimmer's other surviving painting showing a traditional Christian devotional image, his unfinished *Madonna and
Child* (cat. 15).

32. Young Woman (Caroline Hunt Rimmer?)

c. 1874–c. 1877

Oil on canvas, 21 × 17 in. (53.33 × 43.20 cm).
Signed, lower left corner, in red: W Rimmer. Inscribed
in pencil, on front left side of the frame's basepiece:
belongs to Miss Rimmer.

Richard W. Cramer. Bought in February 1976 from
anonymous dealer in Charleston, S.C.

Provenance. CHR; later a private collection in Vermont; later an antique dealer with stores in NYC and
Charleston.

Bibliography. W82, pp. 657–59.

For discussion, see cat. 9 and 37.

33. Picture Buyers

c. 1874–c. 1877

Oil on academy board, 12¹³⁄₁₆ × 9¹⁄₁₆ in. (31.00 × 23.00 cm). Signed, lower right: W. Rimmer. Inscribed, in pencil, on torn MFA label on back: 1–gilded chic—/ 893-glass. Inscribed, in pencil, on back, below MFA label: Picture Buyers–/by/W. Rimmer—/(CHR).

Mr. Marshall Field.

Provenance. Rimmer family, principally CHR; then perhaps ERS. Later acquired by Edward Morrill, Boston, bookseller, and given to his son Samuel, also a Boston bookseller. Sold in 1970 to Clifford A. Kaye, Brookline, Mass. Sold on May 21, 1981, at auction through Robert W. Skinner, Inc., Bolton, Mass., to Jeffrey R. Brown. Sold to Peter Urbon, Deerfield, Mass., then back to Jeffrey R. Brown, Fine Arts, North Amherst, Mass., who sold it to Mr. Marshall Field.

Exhibitions. 1883: Chase, 88. 1916: MFA, lent by CHR.

Bibliography. 1981. Robert W. Skinner, Inc., *American & European Paintings*, sale 740, entry 71. W82, pp. 663–67.

Although on the whole Rimmer's art supports his statement "do not allow yourself to caricature" (Bartlett, *Art Life*, p. 106), there are exceptions. These include an early painting, *The Snuff-Taker*, which may have been a caricature (unfortunately destroyed by Rimmer), and good-natured caricatures of his family made during summer trips. Two drawings from the summer of 1868, *The Wood Chucks* (Fogg Art Museum, 1936.10.51) and *Mountain Climbing Fantasy* (Lincoln Kirstein, NYC), fall into this category, as does the more elaborate drawing from the summer of 1875, *Doing the Mountains on Foot* (cat. 67). Several other drawings with a stronger satirical bite include *Caricature: What We Saw at the Opera* (Fogg Art Museum, 1936.10.16) and *Dedicated to the Massachusetts Society for the Prevention of Cruelty to Animals* (Fogg Art Museum, 1936.10.21).

Other exceptions to Rimmer's statement are the paintings *Picture Buyers* and *The Master Builder* (cat. 27). In *Picture Buyers* Rimmer mocks the false seriousness of pretentious connoisseurs, leaving their relationship to our speculation. The figures' features are striking. The man is related to a number of Rimmer's *Art Anatomy* drawings, particularly to plate 14 of Part I, *The Hair and the Beard and Their Relation to the Physical Constitution*, where drawing 103 is described as "Contradictory Monstrous."

Of all Rimmer's known works, *Picture Buyers* offers the closest parallel to the work of Daumier in both style and theme. This may be only coincidental, both artists having arrived at their particular styles and themes independently through similar training and inclination. Rimmer's particular type of caricature may stem more from the work of Felix O. C. Darley by way of Moritz Retzsch, as well as from the work of, for example, Henry Fuseli. A possible Fuseli influence is also suggested in such paintings as *Scene from "Romeo and Juliet"* (cat. 24) and *The Master Builder*.

It is not known if the pictures on the easel and on the walls in *Picture Buyers* represent actual paintings by Rimmer or by other artists. Although Rimmer did paint a number of landscapes, the easel painting does not appear to be in his landscape style. Rather its style suggests Turner or Thomas Moran. It may even imitate Albert Bierstadt, whose work Rimmer disparaged in several lectures given in Providence during January and February 1873. Whether or not he intended this painting as a comment on the particular type of art displayed, it offers a glimpse of him indulging in unheroic social criticism.

Nearly all Rimmer's caricatures are of secular themes, but there is at least one mythic caricature in his *oeuvre*, his painting *The Master Builder*. The figure and setting have both iconographic and stylistic similarities in Rimmer's work, as well as in works by John Martin and Henry Fuseli. The painting may have a Masonic theme, namely an attack on what Rimmer felt to be an inappropriate externalization of an inter-

nal, spiritual subject. It may also refer to Gnostic myth and depict the demiurge, creator of an evil world in which Rimmer felt himself constantly struggling against insurmountable odds.

In any case, the image is certainly disrespectful. Standing over an abyss, seemingly in command, the figure with its soft, vulnerable body is supported by a precarious structure. This Persian-Assyrian figure type is related to the nineteenth-century interest in Near Eastern culture, seen also in *Flight and Pursuit* (cat. 29). As with many of Rimmer's finest works, *The Master Builder* embraces both personal and universal content.

34. To the Charge (Sketch)/The Battlefield
1874

Oil on cardboard, 12⅛ × 18¼ in. (30.80 × 46.37 cm). Signed, inscribed, and dated, lower right: W. Rimmer/–Sketch 1874. Inscribed, on reverse, in pencil, on label, at upper left: Battle Field–by/ W. Rimmer/Picture injured by him in placing/paper covered with fixitif against/face of painting. This was injured/when doing some work on drawings by/ W. Hunt for Albany Capitol/C H R. Inscribed, on reverse, in black, on label, at upper right: Battle by Dr. William Rimmer/born 1816 died 1879/C H R. ("Battle" is underlined.) Inscribed and signed, on reverse, in pencil, at the bottom: Battle/W. Rimmer. Dated, on the reverse, at the bottom, in pencil, upside down in relation to previous material: Sept 18–70 18–1870. (Since the painting is clearly dated "1874," it is not known to what this date refers.)

Harvard University Art Museums (Fogg Art Museum), 1936.10.1. Purchased in 1936, with the Louise E. Bettens Fund, from the estate of ERS.

Provenance. CHR, then ERS.

Related work. Lost painting *To the Charge/Off to the Charge* (see W82, pp. 673–74).

Exhibitions. Perhaps 1880: MFA, 18, as "Sketch. Landscape with Figures." 1946/47: Whitney/MFA, 22. Apr. 19–June 18, 1972: Fogg Art Museum, *American Art at Harvard*, 78 (ill.).

Bibliography. Bartlett 1882, p. 127. W82, pp. 669–72.

For discussion, see cat. 35.

35. Battle of the Amazons
c. 1875

Oil on canvas, 13⅜ × 18 in. (34.00 × 45.73 cm). Inscribed, in ink, on reverse, on horizontal piece of stretcher: Painted by Dr. Wm. Rimmer/Boston/Given to Louise H. Williams by/C.H.R./1881. (Boston is underlined except for the B.) Labels on back for various owners: Richard Nutt, Dr. Sears, Mr. and Mrs. Gunn, and in various exhibitions: at Yale, the MFA, the 1946 Whitney. Label, on back vertical stretcher: From/F.C. HASTINGS & CO.,/–Importers and Dealers in–/ARTISTS' MATERIALS,/54 and 56 CORNHILL, near COURT ST., BOSTON.

Private collection.

Provenance: First CHR; given in 1881 to Louise H. Williams. Acquired by Dr. G. G. Sears, Boston, and later by Mr. and Mrs. William J. Gunn, Newtonville, Mass. As part of the estate of Marion Raymond Gunn, sold in May 1958 to Richard S. Nutt, Providence, R.I., owner through the mid-1970's.

Exhibitions. 1916: MFA, lent by Dr. G. G. Sears. 1946/47: Whitney/MFA, 21, lent by Mr. and Mrs. W. J. Gunn. Mar. 1–29, 1968: Boston U. School of Fine and Applied Arts, *Boston Painters 1720–1940*, 66, lent by Richard S. Nutt. Apr. 25–June 16, 1968: Yale U. Art Gallery, *American Art from Alumni Collections*, 119 (ill.), lent by Richard S. Nutt.

Bibliography. Bartlett 1882, p. 127. W82, pp. 677–82.

Battle of the Amazons exhibits many of the qualities of Rimmer's mature style: heavily muscled male nudes, emphasis on foreground, action concentrated in the center of the composition, and somber tones highlighted by touches of bright color. The action is depicted at its psychological peak. The spotlighting effect, often inadvertently accentuated by the darkening of bitumen, is another hallmark of Rimmer's mature work, also seen in *At the Window* (cat. 30), *Picture Buyers* (cat. 33), and *Sleeping* (cat. 38). *Battle of the Amazons* appears to have its closest stylistic and thematic affinity with the 1874 oil sketch *To the Charge* (cat. 34). The central horse and foreground figures are especially similar. In fact, the foreground of *Battle of the Amazons* looks like a kind of close-up of the foreground of the 1874 painting. This is fortunate, since the finished painting for which Rimmer's 1874 work is the sketch is lost.

Battle of the Amazons contains heroic male nudes derived from classical and Renaissance sculptures. These aesthetic debts are even more apparent in the 1874 sketch. For example, the torso of the central mounted figure alludes to the *Laocoön* as well as to Rimmer's own *Falling Gladiator* (cat. 5) and *Dying Centaur* (cat. 6). The foreground figures are related to the Elgin marbles, to the *Dying Gaul*, and to Michelangelo's *Day* and *Evening*.

To the Charge is more than a mere textbook exercise in the identification of well-known sculptures or a skillful manipulation of canonical and contemporary sculptural forms transferred to painting. The figures add to the dramatic action and connect Rimmer's work with the heroic artistic ideal he so admired. The painting is small, but its composition and color scheme are lively and exciting. The color of the sky acts as a kind of death pallor, a visual metaphor for the carnage that lies below. Although the costumes suggest an ancient, perhaps Roman, historical or literary subject, Rimmer's oil sketch does not appear to refer to any specific event.

It is, however, possible to identify the specific subject of *Battle of the Amazons*. With the foreground nudes as a heroic setting, the Amazon Queen Penthesilia, with decapitated heads hanging from her horse's saddle, is about to be slain by Achilles as revenge for aiding the Trojans after the death of Hector. According to legend Achilles fell in love with Penthesilia at the moment he killed her. Rimmer has silhouetted Achilles's sword just before the fatal blow, a portent of the ironic reversal to come. Although Rimmer's specific reason for choosing this subject is not known, the legend suggests unfulfilled desire, the despair of loss, and unforeseen, irreversible fate.

Themes derived from Classical literature, ancient history, Shakespearean drama, and the Bible are a hallmark of Rimmer's work, and his interpretations of these subjects often embrace personal symbolism. *Battle of the Amazons* is a fine, mature example in which form, light, and color emphasize the central group. Small though the painting is, its forceful drawing, rich color, and energetic composition create a compelling image.

36. Sunset/Contemplation
1876

Oil on canvas, 28 × 42 in. (71.12 × 106.70 cm).
Signed and dated, lower right corner: W. Rimmer 1876.

Manoogian Collection. Bought from Joan Michelman,
Ltd., NYC, 1984.

Provenance. New England antiques dealer; sold to a
private collector-dealer, thence to Edward Shein,
thence to Joan Michelman, Ltd.

Exhibition. Perhaps 1883: Chase, 91, as "Ideal."

This stunning and until recently unknown work
is Rimmer's only painting dated 1876. Its radiance reflects his improved circumstances during
that year, notably the commission for the *Art
Anatomy* drawings. Although the mood of the
painting is not unusual for Rimmer, the Italian
subject is. The subject and the large size suggest
that the painting may have been commissioned.

At first sight, *Sunset/Contemplation* appears
symmetrical, but closer examination reveals
movement and lively equilibrium. The interplay
of rectilinear and curvilinear forms and the varied disposition of the figures create an enclosed,
controlled, and animated space. The work is also
given vitality by the bold rendering of the animals' anatomy and of the drawing in general.
Since Rimmer never visited Italy, his source may
be a literary one, or he may have been influenced by Claude, Turner, or Allston. The composition, the placement of figures, and the sky
even suggest a stage set.

Above all, the rich tonality of the painting
commands our attention. In the 1870's Rimmer
often used primary and secondary colors to ac-
centuate areas and create a jewel-like glow. He
achieved this through gradations of tone, backlighting, underpainting, and the use of transparent pigments, all of which give his paintings
the illusion of generating their own illumina-
tion. The results, reminiscent of work by Martin
Johnson Heade and Fitz Hugh Lane, suggest
that although Rimmer usually selected different
subjects from these artists, he was not isolated
from his artistic contemporaries. He may have
been directly influenced by their work, or he
may have arrived independently at similar results
through shared concerns.

A mood of introspection predominates in this painting. The time of day depicted, the moment of transition from day to night, implies the fleeting nature of existence. Light envelops everything, with backlighting used to silhouette and generalize the figures. Although the subject is not overtly religious, the work is imbued with a sacred presence.

Sunset/Contemplation eludes attempts at a specific identification of its subject matter, and my title only hints at the work's symbolic import. The painting may be tinged with elegiac content, but it is certainly imbued with a dreamlike ambiance. Rimmer has created a work that exists primarily within the imagination; it stimulates memories, dreams, and reflections. As a landscape of the soul, the picture is both psychologically arresting and aesthetically satisfying.

37. The Shepherd
1877

Oil on canvas, 27 × 22 in. (68.58 × 55.90 cm). Signed and dated, lower left: W. Rimmer./1877. Signed, lower right, below crook: WR.

Label, on back, on bottom stretcher: C HASTINGS & CO.,/–Importers and Dealers in–/ARTISTS' MATERIALS,/54 & 56 CORNHILL, near COURT ST., BOSTON.

Boston Medical Library. Gift of ERS, 1921.

Provenance. Rimmer family, principally CHR; then ERS.

Exhibitions. 1880: MFA, 11. 1883: Chase, 81. 1946/47: Whitney/MFA, 27. 1981: Brockton, 5.

Bibliography. W82, pp. 684–89.

The Shepherd is Rimmer's last dated painting. The concentration on the male torso relates the painting to other works done between 1876 and 1878, including the *Art Anatomy* drawings, especially *The Call to Arms* (cat. 73), the 1877 plaster *Torso* (cat. 8), and the c. 1878 painting *Sleeping* (cat. 38). The rendering of the nude here is particularly successful because the quality of the medium enhances the figure's softness and suggestibility.

Stylistically the painting may owe something to the work of William Morris Hunt, for the palette, like Hunt's, is predominantly subtle, low-toned, and close-valued. Another late painting, *Young Woman (Caroline Hunt Rimmer?)* (cat. 32), suggests an aesthetic affinity both with Hunt and with George Fuller, whose paintings had been popular in Boston since 1876.

The formal qualities of the painting, seemingly straightforward, on closer inspection take on an unsettling aspect owing to the gigantic proportions of the right arm and the peculiar shape of the fingers. The shepherd's crook, almost an afterthought, in fact serves as a counterweight to the figure's massive form.

The near-total nudity of this brooding man relates the work to other examples of Rimmer's talent for anatomical showmanship, but the startling composition and iconographic details add serious overtones to an image that is already provocative. It is possible to view the collar as no more than an extension of the flask's cord—a convenient means of securing this item to a nude figure without distracting visual interruptions. At the same time, however, the collar and the placement of the figure against a rock suggest that the man is in some manner chained to this spot. Rimmer may have intended the figure to have Promethean connotations. The subject remains mysterious but suggestive; as in many of Rimmer's other paintings, a powerful effect is achieved by understatement.

38. Sleeping
c. 1878

Oil on academy board, 8 × 10½ in. (20.35 × 26.68 cm). Signed, lower right: W Rimmer. Inscribed, on back, in pencil, on gray ground, at the top: One of my Dear Father's last [or "best"]/and it is a perfect shame the varnish/is not good and I suppose will be sticky/always. Inscribed on back, below previous inscription, in white paint: Painted by W. Rimmer. Inscribed on back, below previous inscription, in pencil: by W. Rimmer/(CHR). (Rimmer is underlined.)

Kennedy Galleries, NYC. Purchased in 1981 from Leonard and Lisa Baskin, Devon, England.

Provenance. CHR, then ERS. Acquired by Vose Galleries, Boston, and sold in November 1945 to Lincoln Kirstein, NYC. Later owned by Robert Isaacson, NYC; sold to Edward Pawlin, who sold it to Kennedy Galleries, NYC. Sold on Apr. 9, 1974, to Leonard and Lisa Baskin.

Exhibitions. 1916: MFA, lent by CHR. 1946/47: Whitney/MFA, 23, lent by Lincoln Kirstein. Mar. 22–Apr. 8, 1972: Kennedy Galleries, *American Masters 18–19 Century*, 35 (ill.).

Bibliography. W82, pp. 689–96.

Sleeping is one of Rimmer's most evocative works. The style, subject, and verso inscription suggest that it is a mature work. In its portrayal of the child's languid, sensuous form it is similar to two works from 1877, the painting *The Shepherd* (cat. 37) and the plaster cast *Torso* (cat. 8). *Sleeping* also shares certain qualities with *At the Window* (cat. 30) from the mid-1870's: an introspective subject with a dreamlike ambiance enhanced by spotlighting and a setting in which the central figure is surrounded by urns and heavy drapery. The reclining pose and dreamlike state relate the painting to the printed image on the title page of the Rimmer Album (Boston Medical Library), but the nudity and suggestive S-curve of the child's body as well as the painting's revealing light create a different image.

The child resembles young children in paintings by Rimmer from the 1840's and 1850's, figures thought to derive from his own children.

Although Rimmer's daughters were all grown by the 1870's, the child may be a memory image of his youngest daughter, Caroline, who never married, was very close to her father, and was herself an artist. The intimate and provocative treatment of the subject does, however, raise certain questions about Rimmer's intentions, whether concious or not.

The cool color scheme suggests a certain objectivity, but the image of an exposed child with disheveled hair, closed eyes, and open mouth, inexplicably lying on rather than under the bed's heavy covers, has erotic overtones. The drapery, pillows, sheets, and purplish-red coverlet heighten the sultry atmosphere. Any innocence that might be associated with the child's age appears to be contradicted by the picture's revealing light. *Sleeping* is Rimmer's most intensely erotic work. Given what we know of his sensibility as revealed in his writings and choice of subject matter, we must look for an explanation of his intent beyond the Victorian convention of endowing images of children with a mixture of sentimentality and sexuality.

Many aspects of the painting suggest memorial art, notably the vase of flowers, the cool colors, and the fact that the bed is as much an altar for display of the child as a place for her to sleep. *Sleeping* hints at the interrelationships between sleep, unfulfilled desire, and death. It may be a complex metaphor for Rimmer's past and future hopes as symbolically embodied by this memory-fantasy of his daughter or daughters. *Sleeping*, with its allusions to the deathlike state of sleep, may also embody Rimmer's meditations on his own life and death. The painting touches on aspects of Rimmer's life that had been of great importance to him: family, fantasy, death, and anatomy.

Sleeping's fascination partially resides in its symbolic complexity and mysterious nature. Small as the painting is, the enticing image catches our imagination. It is one of Rimmer's most intimate pictures, evocative in its imaginative elements and provocative for its psychological ambivalence.

39. The Gamblers, Plunderers of Castile
1879

Oil on canvas, 14 × 17 in. (35.55 × 43.20 cm).
Signed, lower right, in black paint: Rimmer. Inscribed,
on label formerly on back of frame when painting
was purchased in 1950: The Gamblers/Plunderers of
Castile/by/W. Rimmer/unfinished/owner/C. H.
Rimmer.

Smith College Museum of Art, Northampton, Mass.,
1950.107. Purchased in 1950 from Castano Galleries,
Boston.

Provenance. CHR, then ERS; from her estate to an
unidentified Rimmer family member. Acquired by
Castano Galleries.

Related work. Lost pencil sketch "Gamblers," considered the "First Sketch" for the painting (entry 61 in
1883 Chase Gallery exhibition catalog). See W82,
pp. 1144–45.

Exhibitions: 1880: MFA, 7. 1883: Chase, 84.

Bibliography: W82, pp. 696–700.

The Gamblers, Plunderers of Castile was not
dated by Rimmer, but was documented in the
1880 and 1883 exhibition catalogs as being his
last work, left unfinished at his death. It is one of
Rimmer's most carefully drawn and most meticu-
lously composed pictures. Yet despite the imaginative use of detail, skillful perspective, and
complex composition, the painting lacks vitality.
The action seems too balanced and controlled.
This is partially the result of the overt theatrical
ambiance; the background looks like a theatrical
backdrop, and the actions of the figures appear
to take place on a stage.

The title suggests a specific historical, literary,
or dramatic source of Spanish origin, but the
work has eluded identification. The figures are
stylistically and typologically related to those in
several of the *Art Anatomy* drawings, specifically
to drawing 103, from plate 14 of Part I, an image
described as "monstrous," and to the figures in
two of the drawings from Part II: those in *The
Neck Muscles in Use* (cat. 71) and *The Call
to Arms* (cat. 73). These figures are certainly
not the heroic type of figure so often found in
Rimmer's work.

Because the painting has been documented as
Rimmer's last, it may be in some way related to
the symbolism of the manuscript "Stephen and
Phillip," which preoccupied him at the end of
his life. At the end of this manuscript, (pp. 379
and 381), Rimmer wrote: ". . . there is but one
real difference in men, and it is this. All those
who follow the flesh and live in its gratification,
whether from weakness of conscience or the tyr-
anny of passion are beasts, be they learned or
unlearned, high or low, rich or poor. All those
who master the body and believe in the soul and
the conscience are men, be they who or what
they may."

DRAWINGS AND PRINTS

40. Sacred Subject

c. 1847

Pencil on paper, 12½ × 21½ in. (31.75 × 54.60 cm). Inscribed, on reverse: a very early drawing/my father–W. Rimmer/(C. H. Rimmer).

Kennedy Galleries, NYC. Bought from Robert Schoelkopf Gallery, NYC.

Provenance. CHR. Later owned by Miss Florence D. Snelling, Boston; Lincoln Kirstein, NYC; Robert Isaacson, NYC; Edward Pawlin; The Drawing Shop–Galerie (Osten-Kaschey), now Shepherd Gallery, Associates, NYC; Robert Schoelkopf Gallery.

Bibliography. W82, pp. 753–55.

For discussion see cat. 51.

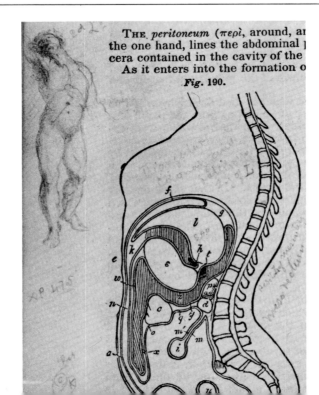

41. Standing Male Nude

c. 1848

Pencil on paper (page of a book), image 2 × ⅝ in. (5.10 × 1.60 cm)

Boston Medical Library. Gift of ERS, 1921, who gave the book in which it is drawn. The drawing is found in the left margin, p. 474, of J. Cruveilhier, *The Anatomy of the Human Body* (New York: Harper & Brothers, 1847).

Provenance. CHR, then ERS.

Bibliography. W82, pp. 755–66.

The figure's contrapposto shows Rimmer's familiarity with Classical and Renaissance art.

42. The Midnight Ride

c. 1853

Pencil on paper, 6 × 7½ in. (15.27 × 19.08 cm).
Inscribed, at the bottom: The/Midnight Ride.

Boston Medical Library. The Rimmer Album, in
which the drawing appears, was given by ERS in 1931,
1932, or 1933. This is the first drawing in the Album.

Provenance. CHR, then ERS.

Bibliography. W82, pp. 759–63.

The Midnight Ride is the first drawing for
Rimmer's poem "The Midnight Ride, a Tale,"
which represents the dark night of the soul. The
Christian resolution is indicated by the cross at
the far right and is borne out at the end of the
poem. Rimmer's image is an early manifestation
of his preoccupation with mythic themes.

---

43. Seated Man

1856

Crayon on paper, 13½ × 10½ in. (34.30 × 26.68 cm).
Signed and dated, at the bottom: W. Rimmer Dec.
17/1856.

Achenbach Foundation for Graphic Arts, The Fine
Arts Museums of San Francisco, 1979.7.85. Gift of
Mr. and Mrs. John D. Rockefeller III, 1979.

Provenance. Private collection, San Francisco. Owned
in 1962 by Victor D. Spark Gallery, NYC, and in 1964
by Mr. and Mrs. Lawrence A. Fleischman. Acquired
by Kennedy Galleries, NYC, and sold Nov. 15, 1967,
to Mr. and Mrs. Rockefeller.

Exhibitions. Feb. 1–Mar. 24, 1964: U. of Arizona Art
Gallery, Tucson, *American Paintings 1765–1963: Se-
lections from the Lawrence A. Fleischman Collection of
American Art*, 84 (ill.).

Bibliography. W82, pp. 767–68.

Depictions of Rimmer's family represent a significant portion of his *oeuvre*, especially in the
graphic medium. The majority of these drawings
represent family members during quiet moments. The sitter here may be one of the artist's
brothers, either Thomas Rimmer, Jr., or George
Rimmer.

Two related drawings share a similar mood
and subject. *Gloucester Shoreline with Seated
Woman* (ill. 13) probably depicts Rimmer's wife
Mary. *Caroline Hunt Rimmer at Wellfleet Beach,
High Tide* (ill. 14) is one of four drawings done
by Rimmer during a family holiday in late
August 1868. In all three works the skillful rendering of texture acts as a foil to the deeply introspective nature of the figures. There is an
element of silence and waiting in these sensitive
portrayals.

ILL. 13. *Gloucester Shoreline with Seated Woman,* 1855. Pencil on paper; 5 × 7 in. (12.71 × 17.85 cm). *Courtesy of the Harvard University Art Museums (Fogg Art Museum).*

ILL. 14. *Caroline Hunt Rimmer at Wellfleet Beach, High Tide,* 1868. Pencil on paper; 11⅝ × 14⅜ in. (29.51 × 36.51 cm). *Courtesy of the Harvard University Art Museums (Fogg Art Museum).*

44. A Border Family
1862

Pencil on paper, 10⅞ × 17⁵⁄₁₆ in. (27.64 × 44.00 cm).
Signed, inscribed, and dated, lower right corner:
Rimmer/Boston/1862. Inscribed, at the bottom, out-
side pencil border: A Border Family.

Harvard University Art Museums (Fogg Art Museum),
1936.10.61. Purchased in 1936, with the Louise E.
Bettens Fund, from the estate of ERS.

Provenance. CHR, then ERS.

Exhibitions. 1883: Chase, 79, 1946/47: Whitney/
MFA, 73.

Bibliography. W82, pp. 783–85.

Rimmer was by no means indifferent to contemporary events. A group of related drawings from
1862–63 showing his reaction to the central
events and consequences of the Civil War is represented in the exhibition by *A Border Family,
The Struggle Between North and South* (cat. 45),
Secessia and Columbia (cat. 46), and *Dedicated
to the 54th Regiment, Massachusetts Volunteers*
(cat. 47). These drawings were inspired by historical situations, and all are essentially political
statements. Rimmer's inventive compositions,
expressive anatomy, and allusive material save
the drawings from becoming static polemics.

A *Border Family* was created as a response to
the civil strife in Kansas and the border states,
a matter of great interest to Abolitionists in
Boston, some of whom were Rimmer's supporters. It depicts a river god nourishing and protecting his young, within a pedimental composition.
The structure imparts a reposeful, timeless quality
to the image. The allusive specificity of this
drawing is somewhat diffused in the larger
Struggle Between North and South, which,
along with its sequel, *Secessia and Columbia,* is
one of Rimmer's most overtly allegorical works.
Struggle reveals Rimmer's artistic sources and his
ability to create his own original forms. One rec-
ognizes the influence of John Flaxman's illustrations for the *Divine Comedy* and the *Iliad,*
Washington Allston's drawings as transmitted by
J. and S. W. Cheney's engravings, David Scott's
mid-century drawings for *The Pilgrim's Progress,*
Moritz Retzsch's illustrations for Schiller's *Lied*

von der Glocke, and Michelangelo's *Last Judgement* and his sculpture *Night.* The large triangular composition provides the setting for a
complex presentation of many figures that are
essentially allegorical embodiments of the main
conflicting factions of the Civil War. Assimilating diverse sources, Rimmer has created an
imaginative and memorable work.

Secessia and Columbia is a polemic; in 1863 it
was distributed in photographic form, with the
proceeds from sales going to benefit the 54th and
55th regiments of Massachusetts volunteers. The
most aesthetically successful of these four drawings, *Dedicated to the 54th Regiment, Massachusetts Volunteers,* was also reproduced and
sold for the cause. Unlike Rimmer's other political drawings, this work possesses a certain kinetic
exuberance that enlivens its polemical nature;
both qualities were acknowledged in the praise it
received.

The 54th Regiment was the first Black regiment mustered into service by the North after

the Emancipation Proclamation was issued on
January 1, 1863. Rimmer's drawing commemo-
rates the regiment's formation in February of that
year. The regiment was subsequently massacred
in the assault on Fort Wagner on July 18, 1863.
The figures cannot be identified as either African
or Caucasian, but the drawing captures the heroic ideal embodied by Robert Gould Shaw, the
regiment's white colonel. Attention is focused on
the animated central group, which calls to mind
Greek hippolytes or Christian soldiers. The figures brandish shields decorated with emblems,
but the principal effect is one of swaying bodies
and heroic unity. The superbly delineated musculature, sensitive shading, and sharp shadows
are powerfully expressive of warlike purpose.
This work is the liveliest and most satisfying
of Rimmer's allegories on the Civil War. For a
more personal response to the theme of war, see
A Dead Soldier (cat. 52).

45. The Struggle Between North and South
1862

Pencil on paper, 16 × 23 in. (40.65 × 58.43 cm).
Signed and dated, lower right corner: W. Rimmer/
1862.

Museum of Fine Arts, Boston. Gift of Edward C.
Cabot, January 31, 1885.

Provenance. Edward C. Cabot.

Exhibitions. 1916: MFA. 1946/47: Whitney/MFA, 39.

Bibliography. W82, pp. 785–88.

For discussion, see cat. 44.

46. Secessia and Columbia
1862

Pencil on paper, 17½ × 24 in. (44.45 × 61.00 cm).
Watermark in the paper: J Whatman/Turkey Mill.
Signed, inscribed, and dated, lower right corner:
W. Rimmer/Boston 1862.

Museum of Fine Arts, Boston, 22.2. Gift of ERS,
Jan. 5, 1922.

Provenance. CHR, then ERS.

Related work. Photogravure copyrighted July 18, 1921,
by A. W. Elson & Co., Belmont, Mass., called "Combat:" examples at Munson-Williams-Proctor Institute,
Utica, N.Y., 66.170, and at Chesterwood, Stockbridge, Mass., 69.38.768.

Exhibitions. Mid-May 1863: Williams and Everett's
Art Gallery, Boston, lent by the artist. C. Mar. 1870:
DeVries, Ibarra & Co., Boston, lent by the artist.
1880: MFA, 51. 1883: Chase, 40. 1916: MFA.
1946/47: Whitney/MFA, 40.

Bibliography. May 13, 1863: "Dr. Rimmer.," *Boston
Evening Transcript.* Tuckerman 1867, 594. C. Mar.
1870: "Fine Arts," *Sunday Herald* (Boston). Bartlett
1880, p. 510. Bartlett 1882, p. 124. Kirstein 1946b,
p. 10. June 1976: Marcia Goldberg, "William
Rimmer's *Flight and Pursuit*: An Allegory of Assassination," *Art Bulletin*, p. 238. W82, pp. 788–91.

For discussion, see cat. 44.

47. Dedicated to the 54th Regiment, Massachusetts Volunteers
1863

Pencil on paper, 17½ × 24½ in. (44.45 × 62.20 cm).
Signed and dated, lower right: W. Rimmer/1863.

Museum of Fine Arts, Boston. Gift of William R.
Ware, Jan. 14, 1909.

Provenance. William R. Ware, Milton, Mass.

Related work. Photogravure copyrighted July 18, 1921,
by A. W. Elson & Co., Belmont, Mass., called "54th.
Mass. Regiment, Memorial": examples at Munson-
Williams-Proctor Institute, Utica, N.Y., 66.172, and
at Chesterwood, Stockbridge, Mass., 69.38.942.

Exhibitions. March to at least mid-May, 1863:
Williams and Everett's Art Gallery, Boston, lent by
the artist. 1880: MFA, 124, lent by William R. Ware.
1946/47: Whitney/MFA, 41 (ill.).

Bibliography. Mar. 27, 1863: C., "A New and Striking
Design. The Dawn of Liberty. Dedicated to the 54th
Regiment of Massachusetts Volunteers. By Dr. Wil-
liam Rimmer.," *The Liberator*, p. 2, column 3.
May 13, 1863: "Dr. Rimmer.," *Boston Evening Tran-
script.* Bartlett 1880, p. 510. Bartlett 1882, p. 123.
W82, pp. 809–15.

For discussion, see cat. 44.

48. Tri-Mountain
c. 1864

Pencil on paper, 7⅜ × 10⅜ in. (18.75 × 26.35 cm).
Signed, lower left: W.R. Inscribed, at bottom center:
Tri Mountain. Inscribed, on reverse: "mat/13/16.

Boston Medical Library. Probably gift of ERS.

Provenance. CHR, then ERS.

Exhibitions. 1880: MFA, 41. 1883: Chase, 33. Mar.
23–June 20, 1981: The Drawing Center, NYC, *Sculptors' Drawings Over Six Centuries, 1400–1950*, 62.

Bibliography. Bartlett 1880, p. 510. Bartlett 1882,
p. 124. W82, pp. 801–4.

Within a single work, Rimmer often explored
variations on a common form. This is seen well
in *Tri-Mountain*, which refers to an early name
for Boston, originally built on three hills. The
drawing is a study for a contemplated monument
to the city. The viewer's attention is engaged by
the composition, by the exposed face of the lefthand figure (which adds a psychological element), and by the forms themselves (which echo
the hill and emerge from it).

49. Bates Sketchbook: Twelve Drawings
1866–1869

Pencil on paper, 10¼ × 8¼ in. (26.05 × 20.95 cm). Stamp, on inside front cover of sketchbook: BOSTON MEDICAL/Jan 28 1921/LIBRARY. Inscribed, at the bottom of the inside front cover: Caroline Hunt Rimmer/from Miss Caroline L.[?] Bates/August–1911.

Boston Medical Library. Probably 1920 gift of ERS.

Provenance. Given by the artist to M. D. Bates. Left to Miss M. L. Bates, and by her to Miss Caroline L. Bates. Given in 1911 to CHR, thence to ERS.

Exhibitions. 1880: MFA, 122, lent by Miss M. L. Bates. 1946/47: Whitney/MFA, 34.

Bibliography. W82, pp. 833–43.

The twelve drawings, each on a separate page in Rimmer's only surviving sketchbook, deal with representative themes from his *oeuvre.* Two of the liveliest ones are reproduced here.

50. Faces: Goth, Greek, Moor

c. 1867

Pencil and brownish ink on paper, with an oval ornamental border (ochre-gilt) printed by lithography. Sheet: 18 × 12¾ in. (45.73 × 32.40 cm). Oval: 11¾ × 9⅜ in. (29.85 × 23.85 cm). Signed, lower right, inside the oval: W. Rimmer. Inscribed, at the bottom, outside the oval, underlined: *Faces*.

Boston Medical Library. Gift of ERS, November 1932.

Provenance. CHR, then ERS.

Exhibitions. 1880: MFA, 4. 1883: Chase, 3. 1981: Brockton, 6.

Bibliography: W82, pp. 847–48.

The most complete and systematic expression of Rimmer's typological interests is found in his *Art Anatomy* drawings (see cat. 68–75), but these concerns pervade his work. This study of three types of man is a particularly fine example; its subtitle comes from the 1883 Chase Gallery exhibition catalog. Although it is undated, the linear style and subject relate it to other work from 1867. The left profile was Rimmer's favorite, and he has given us three interesting heads, both individually and comparatively. This drawing presents a variation on Vitruvian typology. Rimmer's admiration for Greek culture is clearly revealed by his idealization of the Greek figure, which is expressed by the pose, the clarity of line, and the sense of harmony and balance that pervade the composition. The knifelike edge of the Greek figure's helmet and his precise linear profile imply a superiority to the other figures, especially the foreground one with its energized beard. The associations and allusions that this drawing elicit are varied, but they all proclaim the supremacy of the Greek ethos.

A related typological juxtaposition is found in Rimmer's drawing *The Soothsayer* (cat. 65). The sex of this figure is difficult to determine, but it may be male, as is the figure in Rimmer's other *Soothsayer* drawing (Museum of Fine Arts, Boston, 81.100; see W82, pp. 869–870). The

costume of the foreground figure in the exhibited drawing suggests a Roman type, whereas the profile of the background figure implies a Greek one. The figures are contrasted typologically, but there is a psychological bond between them. The vigorous modeling and concentration of the foreground figure express the inspired state of a visionary. The Greek figure's comparative calm suggests that it serves as a daemon for the soothsayer, and by extension for Rimmer.

51. Job and His Comforters
1867

Pencil, pen, and ink on paper, with an oval ornamental border (ochre-gilt) printed by lithography. Sheet: 12¾ × 17⅞ in. (32.40 × 45.40 cm). Oval: 9¼ × 11¾ in. (23.50 × 29.85 cm). Signed and dated, lower right, inside the oval: W. Rimmer 1867. Inscribed, lower left, outside the oval: Job and his/Comforters.

Harvard University Art Museums (Fogg Art Museum), 1936.10.65. Purchased in 1936, with Louise E. Bettens Fund, from the estate of ERS.

Provenance. CHR, then ERS.

Exhibitions. 1880: MFA, 5. 1883: Chase, 4. 1946/47: Whitney/MFA, 74.

Bibliography. June 1976: Marcia Goldberg, "William Rimmer's *Flight and Pursuit*: An Allegory of Assassination," *Art Bulletin*, pp. 234–35. W82, pp. 851–55.

Bartlett tells us that Job was Rimmer's ideal (*Art Life*, p. 95); and whether he was told this by the Rimmer family or whether he deduced it from the artist's work, one can certainly agree. The story of a long-suffering man who was eventually vindicated would have had personal meaning for Rimmer. He treated the Job theme directly in at least one lost painting, *Job and His Comforters* (see W82, pp. 659–61), as well as in several drawings, three of them included in the exhibition.

The first, *Sacred Subject* (cat. 40), from c.1847, is the earliest instance of this theme in Rimmer's *oeuvre*, although the identification of the subject matter is not entirely certain. The textual source is Job 2:13–3:1, just before Job curses his day after he and his three friends have sat together in silence for seven days and seven nights. Job is traditionally surrounded by only three companions; the fourth foreground figure may be an angel or a compositional device. The predominant themes are of grief, despair, and supplication for divine intervention. The arrangement of the figures forms an oval with its rhythmic flow echoed by the tree and a fluid line that relieves the figures' tension. Taken in isolation, each pose might seem contrived, but together they create a mood of solemnity.

The present drawing, made some twenty years later, which is definitely of *Job and His Comforters*, is more complex. Although the figure of Job expresses rage and defiance, the composition is diffuse and overcrowded. There are fine passages in the drawing, but more often than not they are negated by distracting elements. As always, the anatomy is impressive. So is the arrangement of hands and body, which emphasizes the oval composition and creates a gyrating form; but the figure is engulfed and diminished by the huge cloak that silhouettes and isolates it. Many of the incidental elements in this drawing from 1867, as well as Job's basic form, appear to have been borrowed from Blake's *Job* illustrations, especially from the sixth and twelfth plates, although similar incidental elements are also found in Moritz Retzsch's work, which had been an earlier influence on Rimmer from about 1850. Although *Job and His Comforters* lacks the compactness of Blake's images, it does exhibit Rimmer's inventiveness, such as the particularly devilish image of the snake devouring a frog.

And Satan Came Also (ill. 15) is a related drawing from ten years later. It is the only surviving drawing of a group of four, one of which was larger than the others and was dated 1877. They may all have been studies for an even larger drawing or an oil painting. The title comes from *Job* 1:6, in which Satan and the Sons of God present themselves to Jehovah. *And Satan Came Also* seems to be a study of the background action in the largest of the lost drawings. (In Bartlett's *Art Life*, which reproduces all four drawings, the reproduction of this work omits the topmost monster.) This sole surviving drawing is certainly one of Rimmer's most demonic images; and unlike his other depictions of the story of Job, it is wonderfully charged with frenzied energy.

ILL. 15. *And Satan Came Also,* 1877. Pencil on paper; 12½ × 14½ in. (31.75 × 36.85 cm). *Courtesy of the Harvard University Art Museums (Fogg Art Museum).*

52. A Dead Soldier
1867

Pencil on paper, with an oval ornamental border (ochre-gilt) printed by lithography. Sheet: roughly 16¾ × 12⅞ in. (42.55 × 32.70 cm). Oval: 11¹¹⁄₁₆ × 9¼ in. (29.70 × 23.50 cm). Signed at the bottom, within the oval's border: W. Rimmer. Signed, at the bottom of the oval, inside: W. Inscribed, at the bottom, outside the oval: A Dead Soldier.

Museum of Fine Arts, Boston, 81.101. Partly purchased and partly the gift of E. W. Hooper, William S. Bigelow, and Mrs. John M. Forbes, Aug. 8, 1881.

Provenance. Rimmer family, principally CHR.

Exhibitions. 1880: MFA, 9. 1946/47: Whitney/ MFA, 37.

Bibliography. Oct. 30, 1880: F. D. Millet, "The Paintings. The Rimmer Collection," *The American Architect and Building News,* p. 213. Bartlett 1882, pp. 98, 126. 1967: William C. Agee, "Nineteenth-Century Eccentrics and the American Tradition," *The Grand Eccentrics (Art News Annual XXXII),* pp. 135, 149. W82, pp. 855–57.

The events of the Civil War elicited from Rimmer both a public and a private response in the graphic medium. The public response came during the actual years of the war (see *A Border Family,* cat. 44). The private response came predominantly after the war, and is particularly well represented in the exhibition by a group of related drawings from 1867: *A Dead Soldier, The Red Mantle at Pharsalia* (ill. 16), *Philip Preparing the Funeral of Pompey the Great* (cat. 53), and *Achilles* (cat. 54). With varying degrees of specificity, these drawings deal with themes of death, war, betrayal, and assassination. *A Dead Soldier* is related to the other drawings both stylistically and thematically. Through a compositional device Rimmer gives us a dying soldier's view of death. The work has an agonizing immediacy thanks to Rimmer's bold foreshortening and to his placing the vantage point at ground level.

The Red Mantle at Pharsalia and *Philip Preparing the Funeral of Pompey the Great* illustrate episodes in the life of Pompey in Books LXVIII and LXXX of *Plutarch's Lives:* his defeat and his funeral in Egypt. The subject of the first drawing is the red mantle hung by Caesar to signal his intention to fight Pompey in 48 B.C. at what was to be a decisive battle. Since Caesar, by crossing the Rubicon, instigated the civil war against Pompey, who can be viewed as the defender of the Republic, the red mantle alludes symbolically to the Confederate flag and the act of secession. Nevertheless Rimmer's position in the drawing is neutral; his main interest is in the precipitating event of war.

The murder of Pompey, which provides the historical prelude to *Philip Preparing the Funeral of Pompey the Great,* is described in Book LXXIX of *Plutarch's Lives.* After his defeat by Caesar at Pharsalia, Pompey fled to Egypt. Before he could reach the shore, he was murdered in his boat. His freedman Philip wrapped the decapitated body in his own shirt and built a funeral pyre from the wood of an abandoned fishing vessel. Rimmer's drawing depicts the aftermath of the assassination and is faithful to the essentials of the text. The heroic, elevating solemnity of

the imminent funeral is emphasized by the vast landscape and sky as well as by the low vantage point. All the compositional elements direct our attention toward Philip. Rimmer is far from neutral in this drawing, and the symbolic references to the grief following the assassination of President Lincoln are clear.

Achilles is stylistically related to this group of drawings, and it also appears to be related to them thematically, for one of Pompey's three assassins was named Achillas. The emotional scars of war were still important issues in 1867, both for Rimmer and for the nation. He selected classical themes as the means to explore and express his personal response to the national cataclysm. Like the more public allegorical drawings, these were personal works that used myth to universalize contemporary events.

ILL. 16. *The Red Mantle at Pharsalia,* 1867. Pencil, pen, and brown ink on paper with ornamental border; sheet 12¾ × 17¾ in. (32.40 × 45.10 cm). *Courtesy of the Museum of Fine Arts, Boston.*

53. Philip Preparing the Funeral of Pompey the Great
1867

Ink and pencil on paper, with an oval ornamental border (ochre-gilt) printed by lithography. Sheet: 12⅞ × 17¾ in. (32.70 × 45.10 cm). Oval: 10 × 12⁷⁄₁₆ in. (25.40 × 31.60 cm). Signed and dated, lower right, inside the oval: W. Rimmer 1867. Inscribed, lower left, outside the oval: Philip Preparing the funeral of/Pompey the Great—/—In [or "see"] Plutarch.

Harvard University Art Museums (Fogg Art Museum), 1921.27. Gift of ERS, 1921.

Provenance. CHR, then ERS.

Exhibitions. 1880: MFA, 19. 1883: Chase, 16. 1946/47: Whitney/MFA, 75. Jan. 10–Feb. 15, 1959: Addison Gallery of American Art, Phillips Academy, Andover, Mass., *The American Line—100 Years of American Drawing*, 48. Apr. 19–June 18, 1972: Fogg Art Museum *American Art at Harvard*, 77 (ill.).

Bibliography. W82, pp. 861–64.

For discussion, see cat. 52.

54. Achilles
1867

Pencil and pen on paper, with an oval ornamental border (ochre-gilt) printed by lithography. Sheet: 12¾ × 17⅜ in. (32.40 × 44.15 cm). Oval: 9¾ × 11¾ in. (24.80 × 29.85 cm). Signed, lower right, inside the oval: W. Rimmer. Dated, at the bottom, center, inside the oval: 1867. Inscribed, lower left, outside the oval: "But now inglorious, stretch'd along the shore,/They hear the brazen voice of war no more,/No more the foe they face in dire array/Close in his fleet the angry leader lay." (From Alexander Pope's translation of the *Iliad*.) Inscribed, bottom center, outside the oval (to the right of the previous inscription): Iliad.—Book. 11—. (This "11" is merely two vertical lines.) Inscribed, bottom right, outside the oval (to the right of previous inscription): Achilles.

Museum of Fine Arts, Boston, 81.99. Partly purchased and partly the gift of E. W. Hooper, William S. Bigelow, and Mrs. John M. Forbes, Aug. 8, 1881.

Provenance. Rimmer family, principally CHR.

Related work. Photogravure, copyrighted July 18, 1921, by A. W. Elson & Co., Belmont, Mass.: an example is owned by the Munson-Williams-Proctor Institute, Utica, N.Y., 66.168.

Exhibitions. 1880: MFA, 2. 1946/47: Whitney/MFA, 44.

Bibliography. Bartlett 1882, p. 98. W82, pp. 864–68.

For discussion, see cat. 52.

55. The Fencing Lesson
1867

Pencil on paper, with an oval ornamental border (ochre-gilt) printed by lithography. Sheet: 18 × 12¾ in. (45.73 × 32.40 cm). Oval: 11¾ × 9⅜ in. (29.85 × 23.85 cm). Signed, at bottom right, inside the oval: W. Rimmer del. Inscribed, at bottom, outside the oval: "That's his [or "the"] way." / The Fencing Lesson – Showing you how. Label, lower left corner: M.F.A. / No 15.

Boston Medical Library. Probably gift of ERS, in 1931, 1932, or 1933.

Provenance. CHR, then ERS.

Exhibitions. 1880: MFA, 15. 1883: Chase, 12. 1981: Brockton, 2.

Bibliography. W82, pp. 868–69.

Stylistically related to a number of Rimmer's drawings from 1867, *The Fencing Lesson* appears to carry a personal element couched within the framework of a study of nude male soldiers. The inscription, which suggests a specific literary, historical, or biographical content, may allude to the artist's father, who had learned fencing as part of his education and passed this skill on to his children. Whatever the specific subject of the drawing may be, the work displays Rimmer's interest in muscular, foreshortened nudes.
A major influence in this study is the art of Michelangelo. The righthand figure derives specifically from *The Battle of Cassina* as transmitted by Marcantonio Raimondi's engraving.

ILL. 17. *Phillip (Head of a Lion)*, 1869. Pencil on paper; 11⅛ × 7½ in. (28.25 × 19.05 cm). *Courtesy of the Harvard University Art Museums (Fogg Art Museum).*

56. The Duel: "Only the Brave"
1867–1868

Pencil on paper, with an oval ornamental border (ochre-gilt) printed by lithography. Sheet: 18 × 12¾ in. (45.73 × 32.40 cm). Oval: 11¾ × 9⅜ in. (29.85 × 23.88 cm). Signed, lower right, inside the oval: W.R. Inscribed, bottom right, outside the oval: The Duel/"only the brave &cc."

Boston Medical Library. Gift of ERS, end of November 1932.

Provenance. CHR, then ERS.

Exhibitions. 1880: MFA, 54. 1883: Chase, 42.

Bibliography. W82, pp. 881–83.

Rimmer's graphic *oeuvre* is not without naturalistic depictions of male and female lions (e.g., Museum of Fine Arts, Boston, 81.106 and 81.107; see W82 pp. 819–20), but on the whole his images of lions are more symbolic. Rimmer tended to identify with the regal, male lion and used it as a personal and general symbol. *The Duel: "Only the Brave"* takes its title from Laurence Sterne's *Sermons*, Vol. I (1760), no. 12: "Only the brave know how to forgive. / A coward never forgave; it is not in his nature." The drawing appears to be an intimate, symbolic portrait of Rimmer's response to personal crisis, specifically the adverse criticism drawn by his pedagogical program at Cooper Union. The inscription and the composition of the drawing suggest that the lion has literally and metaphorically turned his back on direct confrontation. This lion is complemented by his family circle, much as Rimmer repeatedly sought solace and strength from his own family. The image projects both serenity and strength. In particular, the contrast between the muscular, relaxed body of the male lion and his energized mane suggests internal activity within the context of outward reconciliation and acceptance.

Several overtly charged images are found in *An Old Lion* (cat. 66) and *Phillip (Head of a Lion)* (ill. 17), two of Rimmer's most anthropomorphic works. *An Old Lion* may reflect the increasing problems Rimmer was having at Cooper Union; but whatever its specific stimuli, it embodies the combative arrogance that the artist seems to have himself projected. Its image and its vigorous technique suggest an old pugilist, scarred over many years but with much fight

still left in him. *Phillip* takes its specific inspiration from Rimmer's manuscript "Stephen and Phillip," in which Phillip is a lion consumed by human and by spiritual passion. Rimmer has captured this aspect of his spiritual personality in the flamelike mane, a wrinkled brow, and a tortured expression, and by the treatment of the eyes, described in the manuscript as "glowing orbs" (p. 153).

Although lions appear throughout Rimmer's *oeuvre*, their largest concentration in all media is found between 1869 and 1871 and during 1878. Two examples from November 1878 are his *Dante and Lion* and *Dante and the Lion* (cat. 77 and 78). They take their textual source from Canto I of *The Inferno*, as derived from Thomas William Parsons's *The First Ten Cantos of Dante's Inferno* (Boston: W. T. Ticknor, 1843; reprinted in 1867 with illustrations by Gustave Doré). The thermal energy of both lions' manes is found in other depictions of male lions by Rimmer, most contemporaneously in two from June 1878 (Boston Medical library). In both *Dante* drawings the bodies of the lions are strongly naturalistic, but their overall forms are charged with symbolic power.

The larger drawing appears to be the later of the two. They are both eminently successful, indeed among Rimmer's most memorable graphic images. One is especially struck by the manes: those in both drawings have a burning energy present, but in the later work the mane has gained in substantiality so as to enhance the lion's regal presence. In both works, as in *Philip (Head of a Lion)*, the treatment of the manes suggests an internal ardor approaching religious fervor.

It seems more than fortuitous that both Rimmer and Blake, one of Rimmer's favorite artists, should be inspired by Dante toward the end of their lives. It is also significant that Rimmer's only dated works from 1878 should all be of male lions and should be treated as a vehicle for expressing his spiritual identification with that animal. That the two *Dante* drawings stress the affinity between their human and leonine protagonists, and do so in a heroic manner, shows that they embodied significant symbolic content for Rimmer.

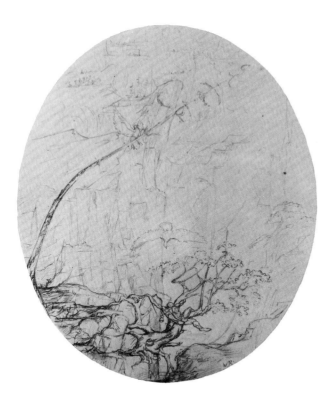

57. Sadak in Search of the Waters of Oblivion
1867–1868

Pencil on paper, with an oval ornamental border (ochre-gilt) printed by lithography. Sheet: 16¾ × 12⅛ in. (42.55 × 30.80 cm). Oval: 11¾ × 9¼ in. (29.85 × 23.50 cm). Signed, lower right, inside the oval: W.R. Inscribed (?), lower left, inside the oval: M A N. (The "N" is in the trunk of the tree, at the base.) Inscribed, at the bottom, outside the oval: Sadak in Search of the/Waters of Oblivion.

Museum of Art, Carnegie Institute, Pittsburgh, 07.10. Purchased in 1907, with Andrew Carnegie Fund, from CHR.

Provenance. CHR.

Related work. Pencil sketch of nude male figure, study for Sadak (Fogg Art Museum, 1936.10.27). See W82, p. 884.

Exhibitions. 1880: MFA, 16. 1883: Chase, 13. 1946/47: Whitney/MFA, 86.

Bibliography: W82, pp. 885–90.

A significant portion of Rimmer's work treats themes of exile and/or quest, of persistence amidst suffering and eventual redemption, themes that embrace personal content within a larger mythic context. Two particularly fine examples in the exhibition are *Sadak in Search of the Waters of Oblivion* and *Knock and It Shall Be Opened* (cat. 58).

Sadak is one of Rimmer's finest drawings, compelling both stylistically and thematically. The story of Sadak comes from a Near Eastern myth, which was transmitted via James Ridley's *Tales of the Genii* (see p. 70). Sadak is sent by the Sultan to find the waters of oblivion, which, when drunk by Sadak's wife, will make her forget her husband, thus allowing the Sultan to seduce her with impunity. Upon Sadak's return, the Sultan grabs the bottle containing the waters and drinks its contents, only to discover that oblivion is death. Sadak regains his wife and is made Sultan. This story is a fitting mythic vehicle for Rimmer's wish for release from poverty and suffering, and for restitution of his rightful inheritance.

Rimmer has presented a symbolic rendition of a Christian myth within the context of this drawing. Sadak's quest takes place in a most desolate and harsh wilderness, with the source of the waters of oblivion not even in sight. In this sense Rimmer's work is quite different from John Martin's earlier popular mezzotint. The sinister setting of Martin's work has been replaced in Rimmer's drawing by a heavenly one. The intensity of Sadak's search is emphasized in Rimmer's drawing by Sadak's expressive anatomy and by the precariousness of his situation. The mountainscape in which he struggles and the tree that seems to entrap him make his search appear hopeless. And yet above his head floats a large bird whose form suggests the dove of the Holy Ghost. This bird, along with the bird on the branch above it, signals the success of Sadak's journey. Because these birds also have small tufts at the back of their heads, it is possible to see them as phoenixes, symbolizing rebirth. The universal character of this drawing is further emphasized by the letters at the base of the oval, which read as "MAN."

The iconic quality of this work is also found in *Knock and It Shall Be Opened*, which takes its textual inspiration from Matthew 7:7. This and the drawing itself leave little doubt that the foreground figure is to be seen as a Christian soldier at the end of his spiritual journey. A primary influence on Rimmer's conception is John Bunyan's *Pilgrim's Progress*. This favorite text of Rimmer also provided material for a number of his other works, including his 1861 sculpture of the *Falling Gladiator* (cat. 5). The affinity between the drawing and the sculpture is further exemplified by the similarity of the forms and close-fitting helmets.

The composition of the drawing reinforces the theme. The figure and landscape elements at the left set this area off from the lighter doorway and from the righthand side of the composition. Thus the figure emerges out of turmoil and darkness into the peace and light of salvation. The wings on the door, positioned above the figure's head, have a symbolic function similar to the bird that hovers over Sadak. Both figures are assured of their just reward.

58. Knock and It Shall Be Opened
1867–1868

Pencil on paper, with an oval ornamental border
(ochre-gilt) printed by lithography. Sheet: 17⅞ × 13¼
in. (45.40 × 33.65 cm). Oval: 11¾ × 9¼ in. (29.85
× 23.50 cm). Signed, at lower right, inside the oval (at
the base of the tree): W.R. Signed, lower right, outside
the oval: W.R. (The letters are joined at the top.) Inscribed, at the bottom, outside the oval: "Knock and it
shall be"/opened.

Boston Medical Library. Probably gift of ERS in 1931,
1932, or 1933.

Provenance. CHR, then ERS.

Exhibition. 1916: MFA.

Bibliography. W82, pp. 890–92.

For discussion, see cat. 57.

59. Draped Male Figure
1867–1868

Pencil on white paper. Sheet: 10⅝ × 5¼ in. (27.00 ×
13.35 cm). Image: 5¼ in. high (13.35 cm). Signed,
lower right: W. Rimmer.

Metropolitan Museum of Art, NYC, 25.122. Gift of
Mrs. George Grey Barnard, NYC, 1925.

Provenance. CHR; later Mrs. George Grey Barnard.

Exhibitions. Perhaps 1880: MFA, 77.

Bibliography. Gardner 1965, p. 14. W82, pp. 895–96.

This figure, which may represent Christ, is almost identical compositionally to the drawing
Classical Figure (Zeus?) from around the same
time (Fogg Art Museum, 1936.10.13). Their
drapery styles, robust form, and severed right
arms suggest that these sculpturally conceived
figures are related to Rimmer's interest during
1867 and 1868 in creating overtly Classical
sculpture. Although the form of *Draped Male
Figure* looks back to Rimmer's statue *Alexander
Hamilton* (frontispiece) and to sketches of a contemplated statue of Peter Cooper (Fogg Art Museum, 1936.10.55–.58), it also looks forward to
his 1869 sculpture *Dying Centaur* (cat. 6).

97

60. Victory
1867–1869

Pen over pencil on paper, 3¾ × 5³⁄₁₆ in. (9.55 ×
13.20 cm). Signed, lower right: W. Rimmer. Inscribed,
at the top: Victory. Inscribed on reverse: "Romantic
Head," split off by Dolloff–B9475 Is Now Drg 60a,
81.109. (This refers to a wash drawing in india ink on
paper, *Head of a Woman in a Hat*, MFA 81.109a; see
W82, pp. 912–13.).

Museum of Fine Arts, Boston, 81.109. Partly purchased and partly the gift of E. W. Hooper, William S.
Bigelow, and Mrs. John M. Forbes, Aug. 8, 1881.

Provenance. Rimmer family, principally CHR.

Related work. Oil painting *Victory* (cat. 26).

Exhibitions. 1880: MFA, 65. 1916: MFA. 1946/47:
Whitney/MFA, 42.

Bibliography. Bartlett 1880, p. 511. Bartlett 1882,
pp. 98, 126. 1977: Graham Hood, Nancy Rivard, and
Kathleen Pyne, "American Paintings Acquired During
the Last Decade," *Bulletin of the Detroit Institute of
Arts*, Vol. 55, No. 2; N.R. (Nancy Rivard) entry on
painting *Victory*, p. 87. W82, pp. 902–4.

For discussion, see cat. 26.

61. Three Figures in a Landscape
c. 1868

Pencil on paper (page of manuscript), 2⅝ × 6½ in.
(6.70 × 16.53 cm). (These are the dimensions of the
image.)

Boston Medical Library. Gift of ERS, 1922. The gift
was the manuscript of "Stephen and Phillip"; the drawing appears on p. 128.

Provenance. CHR, then ERS.

Bibliography. W82, pp. 908–9.

This drawing from Rimmer's unpublished manuscript "Stephen and Phillip" corresponds to the
account of the earthly descent of three angels
described on pp. 85, 87, and 89 of that manuscript. Although the drawing is not fully articulated, it possesses something of the same verve
that characterizes the manuscript's philosophical
content.

62. Creation
1869

Sanguine over pencil on paper, with an oval ornamental border (ochre-gilt) printed by lithography. Sheet: 17¾ × 12¾ in. (45.10 × 32.40 cm). Oval: 11¾ × 9¼ in. (29.85 × 23.50 cm). Signed, in pencil, lower right, inside the oval: W. Rimmer. Signed and dated, at the bottom, inside the oval, in pencil under the sanguine: W. Rimmer/1869.

Harvard University Art Museums (Fogg Art Museum), 1936.10.5. Purchased in 1936, with Louise E. Bettens Fund, from the estate of ERS.

Provenance. CHR, then ERS.

Exhibitions. 1880: MFA, 12. 1883: Chase, 9. 1946/47: Whitney/MFA, 78. June 1972–Apr. 1973: University Art Museum, Berkeley; National Collection of Fine Arts, Washington, D.C.; Dallas Museum of Fine Arts; and Indianapolis Museum of Art, *The Hand and the Spirit: Religious Art in America, 1700–1900,* 90 (ill.).

Bibliography. W82, pp. 946–50.

Rimmer's God the Creator is an impressive figure. A unique instance of this subject in nineteenth-century American art, the drawing depicts the fourth day of Creation, on which God made the sun and the moon. It also appears to refer to the Crucifixion by presenting a second orb and a second crescent shape, located respectively below God's left knee and thigh; the simultaneous appearance of these two heavenly bodies is common in traditional Crucifixion iconography. The triangle above God's head refers to the Trinity.

The massive back and arms that flare out with creative energy echo the form of the triangle. In depicting the figure from the back, Rimmer adheres to the Mosaic tradition that man could not see God's face and live (Exodus 33:20, 23). The beard curls like tongues of flame to create a radiance that recalls Blake's depiction of the Creator God. A similar radiance is an important feature of *Evening, or the Fall of Day* (cat. 63 and ill. 18).

The predominant artistic influence in this work is Michelangelo's fresco of the same subject in the Sistine Chapel. Rimmer combined aspects from each of Michelangelo's two images of God into his own figure. However, the disparity between the back and the leg muscles appears in this context to be Rimmer's symbolic comment on the nature of God the Creator and of God the Son, a merging of Old and New Testament imagery. *Creation* symbolically embodies the active and the passive aspects of God and their reconciliation within His Being. The creative process is anatomically expressed as a combination of action and of gestation, of movement and rest. Similar embodiments of this concern are found in several contemporary works by Rimmer, his sculpture *Dying Centaur* (cat. 6) and his large drawing on canvas *Evening, or the Fall of Day* (ill. 18). It is also possible that Rimmer's figure of God is related to the ambivalent nature of the Deity as found in the Book of Job, a constant source of spiritual and artistic nourishment for the artist.

The symbolic content of *Creation* is reinforced by the composition. The oval shape is a circle in tension; creation is a movement, a contraction out of unity. Other symbolic content in *Creation* may be found with the seven dots within the triangle, which may allude to the seven days of creation and to the stars created on the fourth day. They might also allude to the Pythagorean tradition of the decade and to the sacred numbers seven and three. Many of these symbols are not found within exoteric Christianity, and it is possible that they derive from Rimmer's association with Freemasonry during the second half of the 1860's. By extension, the theme of *Creation* is related to the nature of the artistic process. The particularly leonine character of the beard alludes in part to Rimmer, for whom the male lion was a personal symbol. As a work that presents various levels of content, *Creation* is far more than a copy of Michelangelo.

63. Evening, or the Fall of Day
1869

Pencil and crayon on paper. sheet: 12 9/16 × 14 1/2 in.
(31.90 × 36.85 cm). Image: 11 1/8 × 13 3/8 in. (28.25 ×
31.50 cm). Signed and dated, lower right: W. Rimmer/
1869/Decr 15. Inscribed, at bottom center: Evening.

Museum of Fine Arts, Boston, 59.263. Gift of Miss
Mildred Kennedy, Apr. 9, 1959.

Provenance. CHR, then ERS. Later acquired by Miss
Mildred Kennedy.

Exhibitions. Perhaps c. March 1870: DeVries, Ibarra
& Co., art gallery, Boston, lent by the artist. 1880:
MFA, 52, 59, or 61.

Bibliography. Bartlett 1880, p. 150. W82, pp. 964–65.

For discussion, see ill. 18.

64. Morning
1869

Pencil and crayon on paper. Sheet: 12 9/16 × 14 1/2 in.
(31.90 × 36.85 cm). Image: 11 1/4 × 12 1/2 in. (28.60 ×
31.75 cm). Inscribed and dated, at the bottom: Morn-
ing/Decr 18. Signed and dated, at the bottom, to the
right of previous material: W. Rimmer 1869.

Museum of Fine Arts, Boston, 59.264. Gift of Miss
Mildred Kennedy, Apr. 9, 1959.

Provenance. CHR, then ERS. Later acquired by Miss
Mildred Kennedy.

Exhibitions. 1880: MFA, 10. 1883: Chase, 7. 1916:
MFA, lent by CHR.

Bibliography. Bartlett 1880, p. 510. Bartlett 1882,
p. 125. Kirstein 1946b, catalog entry 15 (for 1869
drawing of *Evening, or the Fall of Day*). W82,
pp. 966–69.

For discussion, see ill. 18.

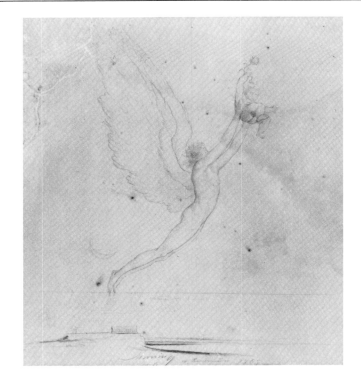

Evening, or the Fall of Day (ill. 18)
1869–1870

Pencil and chalk on canvas, 40 × 50 in. (101.60 × 127.00 cm). Signed, lower right corner, in white chalk: W. Rimmer. Signed, lower right corner, in black chalk, below and slightly to the left of previous signature: W. Rimmer.

Museum of Fine Arts, Boston. 81.110. Partly purchased and partly the gift of E. W. Hooper, William S. Bigelow, and Mrs. John M. Forbes, Aug 8, 1881. Unavailable for exhibition owing to fragile condition.

Provenance: Rimmer family, principally CHR.

Related works. 1866 drypoint (cat. 84). 15, Dec. 1869, pencil and crayon drawing (cat. 63). Dec. 18, 1869, pencil and crayon drawing of *Morning* (cat. 64). July 18, 1921, photogravure copyrighted by A. W. Elson & Co., Belmont, Mass., called "Fall of Day"; examples at Munson-Williams-Proctor Institute, Utica, N.Y., 66.167, and at Chesterwood, Stockbridge, Mass., 69.38.767.

Exhibitions. C. March, 1870: DeVries, Ibarra, & Co., art gallery, Boston. 1880: MFA, 83. 1916: MFA. 1946/47: Whitney/MFA, 15 (ill.). Oct. 9–Dec. 7, 1961: Brooklyn Museum, *The Nude in American Painting*, 6. June 1972–April 1973: University Art Museum, Berkeley; National Collection of Fine Arts, Washington, D.C.; Dallas Museum of Fine Arts; and Indianapolis Museum of Art, *The Hand and the Spirit: Religious Art in America 1700–1900*, 91 (ill.).

Bibliography. Bartlett 1882, pp. 98, 125. Kirstein 1946b, p. 6. 1969: *American Paintings in the Museum of Fine Arts, Boston*, Vol. I, 830, p. 214. Gerdts 1974: p. 102. W82, pp. 969–81.

Perhaps initially conceived as a companion to a now lost painting of *Venus and Cupid*, the drawing *Evening, or the Fall of Day*, although in one sense unfinished, is essentially a fully realized work. The date is based on its first exhibition, on its relationship to the sculpture of the *Dying Centaur* (cat. 6) from the spring of 1869, and most of all on the drawing of *Evening* (cat. 63) dated December 1869 and its companion, *Morn-*

ing (cat. 64). The basic image first appeared in a drypoint dated 1866 (cat. 84). *Evening, or the Fall of Day* is the culmination of these previous images on paper; here the figure has become monumental and articulated. Rimmer has also added a halo behind the head and a blaze of light at the top of the figure's left wing.

Evening, or the Fall of Day is Rimmer's quintessential image, with roots in the work of Michelangelo, Blake, and Doré. Winged, nude, and lacking genitals, the figure is the angel Lucifer, the bringer of light. He eclipses the sun, making it possible also to view him as Satan, the fallen Lucifer. Rimmer's depiction of this archangel does not stress his demonic, Christian aspect but rather his Miltonic qualities of beauty and pride. He is not an evil demon, but a spiritual, daemonic being.

The figure is shown collapsing, vanquished, isolated. The image could be regarded as a metaphor for Rimmer's own artistic difficulties and isolation, for his pride, and for the continual problems he was having with Cooper Union's administrators.

However, the figure's downward lines of movement are balanced by upward sweeping forms. Both the composition and the position of the wings suggest that the figure in fact is hovering in a dynamic equilibrium. The mythic content and beautiful anatomical form seem to express Rimmer's belief in the soul's eternal life. Rather than being a pessimistic image, this work is an expression of spiritual life that endures and transcends the limitations of the physical.

65. The Soothsayer

c. 1870

Pencil on paper, 6⅝ × 9⅝ in. (16.85 × 24.45 cm). Signed, lower right, in pencil: W.R. Inscribed, in ink (?), lower left corner: The Soothsayer by/W. Rimmer——(CHR).

Chelsea Public Library, Chelsea, Mass. Gift of CHR (date not recorded, but before her death, Mar. 3, 1918).

Provenance. CHR.

Bibliography. W82, pp. 936–37.

For discussion, see cat. 50.

66. An Old Lion

c. 1870

Pencil on paper, 9½ × 6¾ in. (24.15 × 17.18 cm). (The paper is of irregular dimensions.) Signed, lower right: W. Rimmer. Inscribed, lower left, underlined: An Old Lion. Stamped, at top left, with M.F.A. label. Inscribed, upper right: Drg/54. (This refers to the 1881 MFA accession, old numbering system.)

Museum of Fine Arts, Boston, 81.103. Partly purchased and partly the gift of E. W. Hooper, William S. Bigelow, and Mrs. John M. Forbes, Aug. 8, 1881.

Provenance. Rimmer family, principally CHR.

Exhibitions. 1880: MFA, 31. 1916: MFA. 1946/47: Whitney/MFA, 38.

Bibliography. W82, pp. 937–38.

For discussion, see cat. 56.

Lion and Mouse (ill. 19)

1871

Pencil on paper. Sheet: 14⅝ × 11⅞ in. (37.15 × 30.20 cm). Image 8½ × 9 in. (21.60 × 22.96 cm). Signed and dated, lower right: W. Rimmer/1871.

Museum of Fine Arts, Boston, 81.104. Partly purchased and partly the gift of E. W. Hooper, William S. Bigelow, and Mrs. John M. Forbes, Aug. 8, 1881. Not available for exhibition owing to fragile condition.

Provenance. Rimmer family, principally CHR.

Related work. Lost oil painting Lion and Snake. See Bartlett 1882, p. 127, illustrated plate XVII; W82, pp. 570–72.

Exhibitions. 1880: MFA, 32. 1916: MFA. 1946/47: Whitney/MFA, 45.

Bibliography. Bartlett 1882, p. 98. W82, pp. 998–99.

For discussion, see cat. 7.

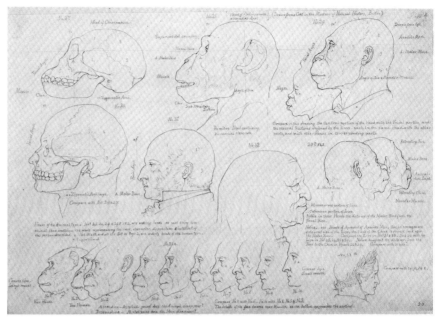

67. Doing the Mountains on Foot
1875

Pencil on paper, 12⅝ × 15¾ in. (32.08 × 40.00 cm). Signed, on pack of lefthand figure: W. Signed, on pack of righthand figure: R. Signed, lower right: W.R. Inscribed and dated, at the bottom center: Doing The Mountains on Foot– August–. Inscribed, lower left corner: Caricature–/In memory of Sights/at Franconia. Dated, lower left corner, next to previous inscription: 1875. Inscribed, lower right corner: No. 1. Inscribed, on the reverse, in pencil: Summer Sketch/of common scene at mountain[s]/Franconia N.H. (C.H.R.).

Harvard University Art Museums (Fogg Art Museum) 1936.10.47. Purchased in 1936, with Louise E. Bettens Fund, from the estate of ERS.

Provenance. CHR, then ERS.

Exhibitions. Perhaps 1880: MFA, 53. Perhaps 1883: Chase, 41. 1946/47: Whitney/MFA, 81.

Bibliography. Perhaps Bartlett 1882, p. 129. Dec. 15, 1968: David Tatham, untitled article, *Appalachia*, n.s., Vol. XXXIV, No. 12, p. 349. W82, pp. 1022–24.

For discussion, see cat. 33.

68. Comparison of Men and Ape Heads
1876

Pencil on paper, 10¾ × 14¾ in. (27.30 × 37.47 cm). Inscribed, top right corner: Page 4. Inscribed, at the bottom: The details of the face become more Manlike as the outline approaches the vertical. Inscribed, lower right corner: 20. Inscribed, at the bottom left: Ascending–At what point does the Animal disappear?/Descending–At what point does the Man disappear?

Museum of Fine Arts, Boston, 19.1461. Acquired on July 17, 1919, as bequest of CHR.

Provenance. Rimmer family, principally CHR; then CHR.

Exhibitions. 1916: MFA. 1946/47: Whitney/MFA, 47.

Bibliography. W82, pp. 1035–36.

In this p. 4 of Part I, "The Skull," from *Art Anatomy*, Rimmer presents an evolutionary scale like Darwin's, delineating the progressive development of ape into man. Drawing 31 is of his father, Thomas Rimmer. Notations to drawing 28 of a chimpanzee indicate that it was drawn from a cast in the Museum of Natural History in Boston; this may have been the Boston Museum, which contained natural history objects, but more likely it was the Warren Museum. The other 30 drawings from Part I delineate, articulate, and analyze the various parts of the head and of the face, investigating through images and text their typological and physiognomic possibilities for artistic expression.

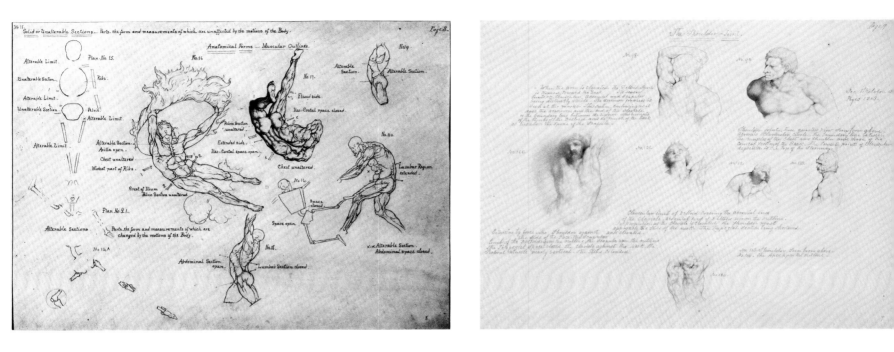

69. The Solid and Unalterable Sections of the Body
1876

Pencil on paper, 10¾ × 15 in. (27.30 × 38.10 cm). Inscribed, upper right corner: Page 3. Inscribed, at the upper left: Solid or Unalterable Sections. – Parts – the form and measurements of which are unaffected by the motions of the Body. ("Solid or Unalterable Sections" is double-underlined.) Inscribed, at the top: Anatomical Forms—Muscular Outlines. ("Anatomical Forms" is double-underlined; "Muscular Outlines" is underlined.) Inscribed, lower right corner: 8.

Museum of Fine Arts, Boston, 19.1491. Acquired on July 17, 1919, as bequest of CHR.

Provenance. Rimmer family, principally CHR; then CHR.

Exhibitions. 1916: MFA. 1946/47: Whitney/MFA, 51.

Bibliography. Mar. 1947: Lincoln Kirstein, "The Rediscovery of William Rimmer," *Magazine of Art*, p. 95. W82, pp. 1065–67.

This p. 3 of Part II, "The Skeleton," follows two rather straightforward presentations of the human skeletal structure. The preceding two drawings and the title of this third hardly prepare the student for the imaginative display with which Rimmer has illustrated his points here. Although some of the stick figures resemble those in Rimmer's 1864 *Elements of Design*, and although the figures at the far right and at the bottom are relatively descriptive in terms of the page's function, it is the two center drawings that catch our imagination.

Drawing 17 alludes to images by Blake as well as to the significant number of falling figures in drawings by Rimmer. Its Miltonic spirit is echoed by drawing 16, Rimmer's Promethean Lucifer. Both scientifically functional and artistically inventive, this sheet early sets the tone for the 50 drawings devoted to the body that constitute "The Skeleton" as well as for most of other *Art Anatomy* drawings.

70. The Shoulder Joint
1876

Pencil on paper, 10¾ × 15 in. (27.30 × 38.10 cm). Inscribed, upper right corner: Page 9. Inscribed, at the top, double-underlined: The Shoulder=Joint.

Museum of Fine Arts, Boston, 19.1497. Acquired on July 17, 1919, as bequest of CHR.

Provenance. Rimmer family, principally CHR; then CHR.

Exhibitions. 1916: MFA. 1946/47: Whitney/MFA, 53.

Bibliography. W82, pp. 1072–73.

In this p. 9 of "The Skeleton," Rimmer's inventive capabilities have been used to complement his material with tonal drawings that dramatically and sensitively illustrate his text. On the whole, the various images suggest poses from life classes. However, drawing 100, at the far left, is also reminiscent of Rimmer's lost painting *Crucifixion* from c. 1847. This page is the culmination of the previous drawings, and a notation at the upper right refers the student to the first three pages of "The Skeleton." The sculptural conception of these figures is a hallmark of *Art Anatomy*.

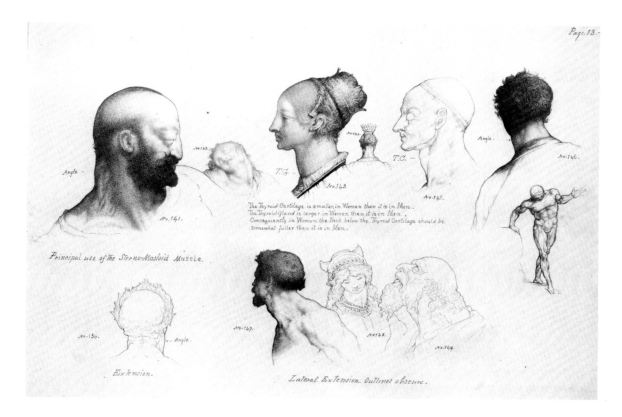

The Thyroid Cartilage is smaller in Women than it is in Men.
The Thyroid Gland is larger in Women than it is in Men.
Consequently in Women the Neck below the Thyroid Cartilage should be
somewhat fuller than it is in Men.

Principal use of the Sterno-Mastoid Muscle.

Extension.

Lateral Extension. Outlines obscure.

71. The Neck Muscles in Use
1876

Pencil on paper, 10¾ × 15 in. (27.30 × 38.10 cm).
Inscribed, upper right corner: Page 13–. Inscribed,
lower right corner: 11.

Museum of Fine Arts, Boston, 19.1501. Acquired on
July 17, 1919, as bequest of CHR.

Provenance. Rimmer family, principally CHR; then
CHR.

Exhibitions. 1916: MFA. 1946/47: Whitney/MFA,
55. Sept. 2–Oct. 24, 1976: Minneapolis Institute of
Arts, 108; Nov. 23, 1976–Jan. 23, 1977: Whitney
Museum of American Art, 111; Feb. 19–Apr. 1, 1977:
The Fine Arts Museums of San Francisco, The Cali-
fornia Palace of the Legion of Honor, 110, *American
Master Drawings and Watercolors* (ill.).

Bibliography. W82, pp. 1076–78.

This p. 13 of Part II, "The Skeleton," like pp. 3
and 9 (cat. 69 and 70), introduces the student to
the creative possibilities inherent in a combination of anatomical study and artistic creation.
Combining line and tonal images, the drawings
show Rimmer's debt to Classical and other
sources, allude to his interest in the theater, and
remind the student of the wonderful heads from
Part I, "The Skull." This page is a delight, providing an imaginative rest from the wealth of
material that precedes it and clearly demonstrat-
ing the superiority of artistic anatomy over mere
delineation of anatomical forms.

72. The Pectoralis Major in Use
1876

Pencil on paper, 10¾ × 15 in. (27.30 × 38.10 cm).
Inscribed, upper right corner: Page 23. Inscribed,
lower right: . . . When the muscles are full, the integu-
ment is full:/When the muscles are thin, the integu-
ment is thin./(Male proportions.)

Museum of Fine Arts, Boston, 19.1511. Acquired on
July 17, 1919, as bequest of CHR.

Provenance. Rimmer family, principally CHR; then
CHR.

Exhibitions. 1916: MFA. 1946/47: Whitney/MFA,
61.

Bibliography. W82, pp. 1087–88.

This beautifully drawn figure from p. 23 of Part
II, "The Skeleton," occupies the most complete
composition that the student has yet encountered in *Art Anatomy,* even though all the pages
have a compositional integrity. The figures and
surrounding objects relate this drawing to p. 26,
The Call to Arms (cat. 73).

An earlier work with a similar use of a curving
anatomical form and a hand holding an object
in the foreground is found in the drawing
Achilles (cat. 54) from 1867. This form is also
found in the 1863 drawing *Dedicated to the 54th
Regiment, Massachusetts Volunteers* (cat. 47). It
was evidently one that Rimmer found particularly expressive and capable of being explored in
a number of variations. Like pp. 9 and 13 of *Art
Anatomy* (cat. 70 and 71), this drawing offers a
summation of the structural aspects of the re-
spective muscles and is dramatic evidence of the
possibilities of artistic anatomy.

ILL. 20. *Nude Males*, 1873. Pencil on paper; 11¹⁵/₁₆ × 14½ in. (30.35 × 36.85 cm). *Courtesy of the Harvard University Art Museums (Fogg Art Museum)*.

73. The Call to Arms
1876

Pencil on paper, 10¾ × 15¼ in. (27.30 × 38.73 cm). Signed and dated, lower right corner: W. Rimmer 1876. (There are faint indications of a second "W" above the "R.") Inscribed, upper right corner: Page 26.

Museum of Fine Arts, Boston, 19.1514. Acquired on July 17, 1919, as bequest of CHR.

Provenance Rimmer family, principally CHR; then CHR.

Exhibitions. 1880: MFA, 43. 1916: MFA. 1946/47: Whitney/MFA, 62. Sept. 2–Oct. 24, 1976: Minneapolis Institute of Arts, 109; Nov. 23, 1976–Jan. 23, 1977: Whitney Museum of American Art, 112; Feb. 19–April 1, 1977: The Fine Arts Museums of San Francisco, The California Palace of the Legion of Honor, 111, *American Master Drawings and Watercolors* (ill.).

Bibliography. Bartlett 1880, pp. 510, 511. Bartlett 1882, pp. 86, 124. Mar. 1947: Lincoln Kirstein, "The Rediscovery of William Rimmer," *Magazine of Art*, p. 95. W82, pp. 1090–93.

This p. 26 of Part II, "The Skeleton," is the only one of the 81 *Art Anatomy* drawings that is signed and dated, being conceived as a full-fledged composition. The Contents pages for *Art Anatomy* describe this page simply as a "full-page drawing, illustrating muscular development." Although it does superficially fit this description by depicting the rectus abdominis and the obliquus externus muscles, the drawing is a startling revelation to the student because it displays the artistic possibilities inherent in the study of artistic anatomy.

The Call to Arms presents a kind of compendium of forms and themes that are found throughout Rimmer's work. Its figures are reminiscent of those in his 1862 drawing *The Struggle Between North and South* (cat. 45), the 1867 drawing *Achilles* (cat. 54), the 1873 drawing *Nude Males* (ill. 20), a lost painting titled *Soldiers by a Stream*, the 1877 painting *The Shepherd* (cat. 37) and the sculpture *Torso* (cat.

8). They also recall figures in works by Moritz Retzsch, Washington Allston, William Blake, and Michelangelo.

Although the theme of *The Call to Arms* was treated in stone by François Rude in *La Marseillaise* of 1833–36 on the Arc de Triomphe, there is no indication that Rimmer's drawing refers to that work or to any specific literary or mythological source. Rather it is related to general mythological and Classical sources from which Rimmer constantly drew inspiration. Fusing many elements into one memorable image, *The Call to Arms* would certainly inspire any student of artistic anatomy.

74. Female Proportions
1876

Pencil on paper, 10½ × 14⅜ in. (26.88 × 36.50 cm). Inscribed, upper right corner: Page 47. Inscribed, at the top, double-underlined: Female Proportions.

Museum of Fine Arts, Boston, 19.1535. Acquired on July 17, 1919, as bequest of CHR.

Provenance. Rimmer family, principally CHR; then CHR.

Exhibitions. 1916: MFA. 1946/47: Whitney/MFA, 69.

Bibliography. W82, pp. 1110–11.

This p. 47 of "The Skeleton" illustrates Rimmer's feminine canon. Conceived as Classical sculptural fragments, these figures, like so many others in *Art Anatomy*, clearly demonstrate the sculptural conception of the work.

75. Foreshortening
1876

Pencil on paper, 10½ × 14⅜ in. (26.68 × 36.50 cm). Inscribed, upper right corner: Page 50. Inscribed, at the top, double-underlined: Fore-Shortening. Inscribed, at the bottom: No. 280. When such parts of the body as are not fore-shortened cover other parts, which from the character of the position must be fore-shortened, if seen, / the truthfulness of the fore-shortening will depend upon the accuracy of the projecting part in relation to the supposed place of the part obscured. / Fore-shortening of this discription [*sic*] may be known as Fore-shortening by obscuration.

Museum of Fine Arts, Boston, 19.1538. Acquired on July 17, 1919, as bequest of CHR.

Provenance. Rimmer family, principally CHR; then CHR.

Exhibitions. 1916: MFA. 1946/47: Whitney/MFA, 71.

Bibliography. W82, pp. 1113–15.

This fiftieth and final drawing of Part II, "The Skeleton," is one of two specifically described as dealing with foreshortening, although many of the drawings of the head from Part I, "The Skull," and of the body from "The Skeleton" have foreshortened images. As with many of the other *Art Anatomy* drawings, this page offers the student examples of the creative possibilities inherent in engaging in this study. Although *The Call to Arms* (cat. 73) can be related in a general manner to Rimmer's essential thematic concerns, the individual drawings on this final page of *Art Anatomy* encompass a wide variety of subjects and themes and are encapsulations of Rimmer's thematic interests, representing a kind of overview of his symbolic concerns. They are essentially indicative of universal material, but they also embrace personal meaning.

The top left image suggests aristocratic and theatrical themes, and the top right figure might represent the exiled or questing Christian from Bunyan's *Pilgrim's Progress* or Sadak from Ridley's *Tales of the Genii*, with many variants in

Rimmer's *oeuvre*. The broken cross and figure at bottom left might very well carry both a personal and a religious message. Most of Rimmer's works have religious content, whether explicitly or not; he himself remarked that it was always "his desire to deal with Scriptural subjects in this art" (Bartlett, *Art Life*, p. 95). The next drawing to the right, of a winged figure, is one of many Luciferian beings in Rimmer's works, who may be metaphors for the artist or be more general representations of spirituality. The two putti, one chasing a butterfly, the other holding a torch, might symbolize the innocence of childhood or the untarnished soul before it is born into the body. Romantic yearnings in the Wordsworthian manner pervade Rimmer's work. At the far right, we see a Golden Age: Rimmer's mythic concept embodied in the ideal nude.

76. The Shepherd

c. 1877

Pastel over pencil on brown-washed paper treated with fixative, 14 × 21¼ in. (35.55 × 54.00 cm). Label, on back of former frame: 'The Shepherd'/by Dr. William [Rimmer]/Property of Miss S. Minns/14 Louisburg Sq. Boston. Label, on back of former frame, has information on the 1916 MFA exhibition.

The Art Museum, Princeton University, 50.40. Gift of Frank Jewett Mather, Jr., 1950.

Provenance. Miss Susan Minns, Boston. Acquired by Castano Galleries, Boston, and sold in the summer of 1950 to Frank Jewett Mather, Jr., Princeton, N.J.

Related work. Photogravure copyrighted July 18, 1921, by A. W. Elson & Co., Belmont, Mass.; an example is owned by the Munson-Williams-Proctor Institute, Utica, N.Y., 66. 169.

Exhibitions. 1880: MFA, 60, lent by Miss Susan Minns. 1916: MFA, lent by Miss Susan Minns.

Bibliography. 1976: Barbara T. Ross, *Amerian Drawings in the Art Museum, Princeton University*, p. 113. W82, pp. 806–9.

Rimmer's preoccupation with the heavily muscled male nude is well-represented by works in the exhibition. *The Shepherd* is one of his finest renderings of the figure seen from the back. Iconographically related to his 1877 painting *The Shepherd* (cat. 37), the figure in the pastel, whose face is hidden, represents a less psychologically complex but no less compositionally interesting figure. Although the anatomy is magnificently rendered, there is a certain anomaly or incongruity between the flat upper back and the sculptural treatment of the lower back, an incongruity that is heightened by the flattening of space due to the scale, the positions of the sheep, and the outlines. A visual compression of the middle ground, achieved by various means, is often found in Rimmer's work, two earlier examples being his lithograph *The Roarers* (cat. 80) and his drawing *Sadak in Search of the Waters of Oblivion* (cat. 57). A tension is created in the pastel that appears to contradict the relaxed outline of the figure. This visual excitement is increased by the low vantage point, which brings the background forward and helps to involve the viewer in the work.

109

77. Dante and Lion
1878

Pencil on paper, 10¹¹⁄₁₆ × 13⅜ in. (27.20 × 33.90 cm). Dated and signed, at lower left: 1878 W. Rimmer. Inscribed, lower right, in pencil: "But soon a lion met my startled sight, –/Whose fearful shape renewed my late distress./With towering head he stalked and ravenous mien."/Canto 1st/Lines xxxv.xxxvi.xxxvii. Inscribed, lower right, in ink, below previous material: The time was morning, and the Sun above/The world was riding with his Kindred stars,/T. W. Parsons.

Wadsworth Atheneum, Hartford, Conn., 1979.187. Purchased in October 1979 with James J. Goodwin Fund, from Vose Galleries, Boston.

Provenance: CHR (?), then ERS(?). Acquired by Frank Crowley, Jr. and sold in April 1979 to Vose Galleries.

Bibliography: W82, pp. 1175–80.

For discussion, see cat. 56.

78. Dante and the Lion
1878

Pencil on paper, 5¾–6⅛ × 9⁷⁄₁₆ in. (14.61–15.59 × 24.00 cm); these are the dimensions of the irregular paper. The dimensions of the darker area on the sheet that contains the image: 5½ × 9 in. (14.00 × 22.96 cm). Signed and dated, at the lower right: W. Rimmer Nov./'78. Inscribed, at the lower right corner: Illustrating passage from Dante's Inferno. ("Dante's Inferno" is underlined except for "Da.") Inscribed, in the upper left margin, with what appears to be a "4" on its side.

Museum of Fine Arts, Boston, 81.105. Partly purchased and partly the gift of E. W. Hooper, William S. Bigelow, and Mrs. John M. Forbes, Aug. 8, 1881.

Provenance. Rimmer family, principally CHR.

Exhibitions. 1880: MFA, 37. 1916: MFA, 1946/47: Whitney/MFA, 46.

Bibliography. W82, pp. 1140–44.

For discussion, see cat. 56.

79. The Fireman's Call
1837

Lithograph (music cover). Sheet: 13⅛ × 10 in. (33.33 × 25.42 cm). Image: 7⅛ × 8¾ in. (18.12 × 22.25 cm). Signed, lower left, outside the image (in the stone): W. Rimmer, del. Inscribed (printed) below the image: THE FIREMAN'S CALL, / As Sung by / GEORGE WASHINGTON DIXON, / Respectfully Dedicated to the Officers and Members of the / Fire Department of Boston. / Music from the Opera of the Maid of Judah. / Boston: Published by C. H. Keith, 67 Court Street. / Entered according to Act of Congress in the Year 1837, by C. H. Keith, in the Clerk's Office of the / District Court of Massachusetts.

American Antiquarian Society, Worcester, Mass.

Provenance. None recorded.

Related works. There are two other known prints with the signature, in the collections of the Harvard College Library and of S. Grant Waters. Two examples of the lithograph without the signature are known, both from 1845: they are in the Boston Public Library and the Starr Music Collection (box on "Disasters"), Lilly Library, Indiana University, Bloomington, Ind. The dimensions of the variant are slightly larger than those of the signed lithograph.

Exhibitions. 1946/47: Whitney/MFA, 88. Apr. 7–May 16, 1976: Worcester Art Museum, *New England Prints Before 1850*, 56.

Bibliography. Bartlett 1882, p. 9. 1973: David Tatham, *The Lure of the Striped Pig: The Illustration of Popular Music in America, 1820–1870*, p. 60; the illustration is the print at the Harvard College Library. W82, pp. 739–41.

During 1837 Rimmer worked in Thomas Moore's lithographic shop and shortly thereafter in Daniel Jenkins's lithographic shop, both in Boston. The year before, Moore had purchased the shop of John and William Pendelton, two brothers who established the first lithographic firm in the United States in Boston during the mid-1820's. Two examples survive of Rimmer's earliest work in lithography, *The Fireman's Call*, done for and printed by Moore, and *The Roarers* (cat. 80), most probably put on stone for Jenkins. Both are sheet music covers, both lack the refinement of similar work by contemporaries, and both are informed by Rimmer's membership in such civic organizations as Fire Engine Company No. 12 and the City Guards.

The discrepancy in style and technique between these two works and a slightly earlier lithograph by Rimmer, *Le Chien du Chasseur*, which though lost is known from an illustration in Bartlett's *Art Life*, is puzzling. The high quality and expert draughtsmanship of the lost work, which may not have been a sheet music cover, is absent in the surviving lithographs. This may be partially explained by the less than inspiring quality of the songs that provided Rimmer's material. However, Rimmer's evident difficulty in depicting the foot of the woman in *The Fireman's Call* occurred again more than ten years later in his painting of *Scene from "Macbeth"* (cat. 17).

Whether the stylistic awkwardness was due to simplification or lack of skill, both sheet music covers nonetheless have a lively effect. *The Fireman's Call* is invested with a boldness and urgency appropriate to its subject; the plunging perspective, the contrasts of shape and texture, and the use of light and dark enliven the dramatic scene. Similarly, in *The Roarers* the primitive style is well-suited to raucous self-proclamation by the foreground lion, the insignia of the Rifle Rangers, to whom the song was dedicated. The oval design, echoed by the cave and by the lion's form, contributes to the activated effect.

The Roarers presents Rimmer's earliest known image of a lion. Similar in form to the dog in the lost *Le Chien du Chasseur*, this lion is in a combative pose. Because the male lion became a personal symbol for Rimmer, its earliest appearance is of particular interest. The spatial arrangement of *The Roarers* is an instance of the composition Rimmer would later use in many of his drawings and paintings: main action in the foreground, distant activity with minute figures in the background, and a relatively compressed middle ground. The interplay of light and dark values that appears frequently in Rimmer's paintings was initially explored in his lithographs. The sheet music covers were most likely given to Rimmer as routine assignments, but they already show him developing his own recognizable style.

80. The Roarers
1837

Lithograph (music cover). Sheet: 13¼ × 9⅞ in. (33.67 × 25.10 cm). Image: 7⅞ × 9½ in. (20.01 × 24.15 cm). Signed, lower left, near edge of image (in the stone): W. Rimmer del. Inscribed, lower right, near edge of image: Jenkins' Lith. Inscribed (printed) below the image: THE ROARERS. / A Quick Step, Composed Expressly for the / Rifle Rangers / And Humbly Dedicated to / CAPT. CHARLES C. PAINE, / OFFICERS and MEMBERS of the R. R. BOSTON, / BY JOHN HOLLOWAY. / Performed for the first time by the Boston Brass Band at Holloway's Farewell Concert, March 11, 1837. / Boston: Published by Chs. H. Keith, 67 Court Street.

American Antiquarian Society, Worcester, Mass.

Provenance. None recorded.

Related work. One other print with the signature is in the collection of the Harvard College Library.

Exhibitions. 1946/47: Whitney / MFA, 89. Apr. 7–May 16, 1976: Worcester Art Museum, *New England Prints Before 1850,* 55.

Bibliography. 1973: David Tatham, *The Lure of the Striped Pig: The Illustration of Popular Music in America, 1820–1870,* p. 58; the illustration is the print at the Harvard College Library. W82, pp. 741–43.

For discussion, see cat. 79.

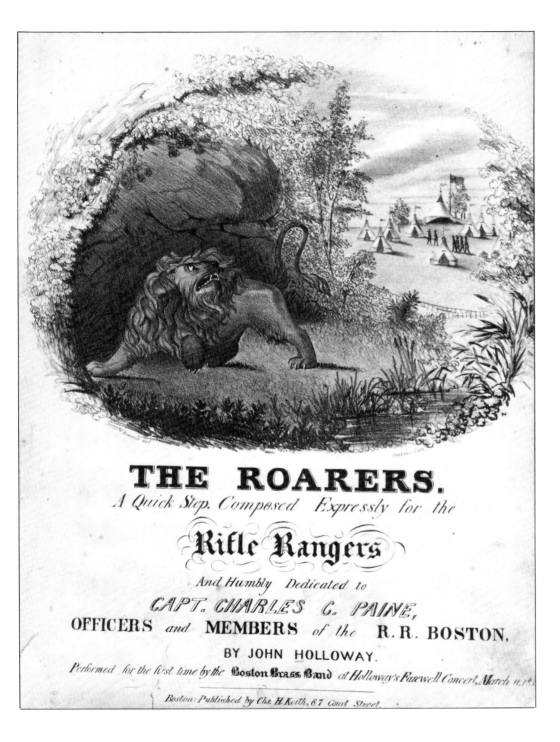

THE ROARERS.

A Quick Step, Composed Expressly for the

Rifle Rangers

And Humbly Dedicated to

CAPT. CHARLES C. PAINE,

OFFICERS *and* MEMBERS *of the* R. R. BOSTON,

BY JOHN HOLLOWAY.

Performed for the first time by the Boston Brass Band *at Holloway's Farewell Concert, March 11, 18...*

Boston: Published by Chs. H. Keith, 67 Court Street.

81. Head of a Prophet (?)

c. 1845

Lithograph, 6³⁄₁₆ × 4¾ in. (17.75 × 12.09 cm).

Worcester Art Museum, Goodspeed Collection (G 2590). Purchased in 1910 as part of a collection of over three thousand early American prints from Charles Goodspeed, Boston.

Provenance. Charles Goodspeed.

Exhibitions. Apr. 7–May 16, 1976: Worcester Art Museum, *New England Prints Before 1850,* 57. Sept. 24, 1976–Jan. 23, 1977: Worcester Art Museum, *The Second Fifty Years: American Art, 1826–1876,* 79.

Bibliography. W82, pp. 747–48.

Head of a Prophet(?) and *The Entombment* (cat. 82) represent Rimmer's return to lithography, a medium he had not touched since 1837. Their relatively small size and their subjects suggest the possibility that they were created for distribution to the pious, perhaps within the context of a church fair. Whether deliberately or because Rimmer lacked skill as a lithographer, both works exhibit the stylistic simplification and primitive exuberance found in his earlier lithographs.

Both works vigorously exploit the contrast of light and dark values inherent in the medium. In *Head of a Prophet(?)* the treatment functions as a symbolic equivalent to the figure's ecstatic state as he awakens from darkness into spiritual light. Within a very small format Rimmer created a charged image, one that suggests the influence of Washington Allston's work.

The robust figures in *The Entombment* are heroic and transform the several awkwardly drawn areas into a forceful image. Also the composition is enlivened by the inventive and somewhat tortuous figure of Christ. Rimmer's image appears to be a traditional one, perhaps deriving from prints in the Boston Museum. Like *Head of a Prophet(?),* *The Entombment* is a powerful image despite its small size.

82. The Entombment
1845

Lithograph. Image, including border: 1¹³⁄₁₆ × 5¹¹⁄₁₆ in. (12.25 × 14.45 cm). Signed and dated, in pencil, lower left, between the image and the border: W. Rimmer 1845.

Worcester Art Museum, Goodspeed Collection (G 2589). Purchased in 1910 as part of a collection of over three thousand early American prints from Charles Goodspeed, Boston.

Provenance. Charles Goodspeed.

Exhibitions. Apr. 7–May 16, 1976: Worcester Art Museum, *New England Prints Before 1850*, 58. Sept. 24, 1976–Jan. 23, 1977: Worcester Art Museum, *The Second Fifty Years: American Art, 1826–1876*, 78.

Bibliography. W82, pp. 749–51.

For discussion, see cat. 81.

83. Reclining Female Nude

c. 1858

Lithograph. Sheet: 11⅛ × 15⅞ in. (28.25 × 40.30 cm). Image: 10⅛ × 10⅞ in. (25.70 × 27.64 cm). Signed, lower left corner (in the stone): R.

Museum of Fine Arts, Boston, M7393. Gift of CHR, 1891.

Provenance. CHR.

Exhibitions. 1946/47: Whitney/MFA, 91. Apr. 12–June 15, 1975: MFA, *American Prints, 1813–1913*, 28.

Bibliography. 1974: Carl Zigrosser, *Prints and Their Creators*, p. 90. 1976: Fritz Eichenberg, *The Art of the Print*, pp. 416, 417. W82, pp. 769–71.

Rimmer's reasons for doing this work are not known, but he may have been encouraged by Stephen Perkins to return to lithography, a medium he had not explored since the mid-1840's. The specific subject is not easily discerned; it may be a general allegory on the theme of indulgence. Although technically accomplished, this lithograph, the last Rimmer is known to have done, possesses little of the verve of his earlier work.

84. Evening, or the Fall of Day
1866

Drypoint, 3⅛ × 4¹⁵⁄₁₆ in. (7.95 × 12.55 cm). Signed and dated, at left (in the plate): W.R. / 1866.

Boston Medical Library. Probably gift of ERS in 1931, 1932, or 1933.

Provenance. CHR, then ERS.

Related work. A second impression is at the MFA, 81.108; partly purchased and partly the gift of E. W. Hooper, William S. Bigelow, and Mrs. John M. Forbes, Aug. 8, 1881. For later works with the same image, see cat. 63 and ill. 18, p. 101.

Exhibitions. Perhaps 1880: MFA, 52, 59, or 61. 1916: MFA.

Bibliography. W82, pp. 828–31.

For discussion, see ill. 18.

85. The Poor Man Has Nothing to Lose
1878

Proof of linocut after a drawing. Image, including border: 8⅛ × 7¹/₁₆ in. (20.65 × 17.98 cm). Signed, at the lower right (in the plate): Zeros. Inscribed (printed), at the bottom, outside the enclosing border in the plate: "The Poor Man has nothing to lose." Signed, in pencil, lower left corner, outside the enclosing border in the plate: W.R. Inscribed, on the reverse, in pencil: Drawn by W. Rimmer is sketch for paper [newspaper] on which (his son-in-law) happened to be working & at his request. Inscribed, on the reverse, at the bottom: Drawn By W. Rimmer as a sketch/for paper on which(his son in law)/happened to be working and at his request. (Owing to framing, the two inscriptions on the reverse are not now visible. The line breaks in the first and the medium of the second are not recorded, and the duplication is unexplained. The parentheses are part of the inscriptions as recorded.)

Private collection. Gift from Miss Florence D. Snelling, ca. 1958.

Provenance. CHR; given to Miss Florence D. Snelling, Boston.

Exhibition. 1946/1947: Whitney/MFA, 94.

Bibliography. 1878: *The Porcupine*, reproduction, probably without Rimmer's initials at the lower left from the proof. Bartlett 1882, p. 126. W82, pp. 1131–36.

The Poor Man Has Nothing to Lose, an example of Rimmer's sympathy for the impoverished, expresses his concern for the workers during the labor problems of 1878 in Fall River, Massachusetts, who were said by the press to have nothing to lose while the capitalists staked everything. It was executed at the request of his son-in-law, William O. Haskell, joint-editor of *The Porcupine*, a short-lived newspaper or periodical. Rimmer may have signed the work as Zeros to avoid charges of nepotism or repercussions that might affect his position at the School of the Museum of Fine Arts.

Although the print relates to a specific historical event, the subject has been idealized and universalized. Rimmer's Christian Transcendentalism and Christian Socialism are couched within a mythic mold. Here the family unit is emphasized by the strong triangular composition with the male at the apex, a device used by Rimmer for a related purpose in a drawing of 1862, *A Border Family* (cat. 44). The emphasis on closeness of family in Rimmer's 1878 work is found in the second to last plate from Blake's *Job*, an image that embraces both the familial and the angelic aspects of Rimmer's later print. The form of Rimmer's angel is also found in a number of works by Blake, among them *Glad Day*.

The robust solidarity of family in Rimmer's work expresses endurance. Permanence and monumentality are implied by a pyramidal composition. The empty foreground creates a hallowed atmosphere; and this, together with the protecting angel, sanctifies the group. The man wears a Roman cuirass, and his general form can be related to Horatio Greenough's 1832–41 statue *George Washington* (Smithsonian Institution). Rimmer has created an image of the Christian soldier and endowed him with the virtues of Republican Rome and the support of a contemporary American family.

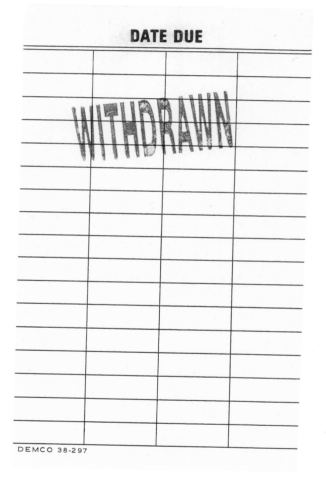

DATE DUE

WITHDRAWN